Symbolic Images in Art As Therapy

In *Symbolic Images in Art As Therapy* **R.M. Simon** highlights the contribution both art and the art of the therapist can make in working to ease the effects of bereavement, depression, abuse, physical handicap or other causes of mental distress. Combining detailed case material and over eighty examples of patients' work, the author discusses the style in which images are produced and shows how a transition from one style to another relates to a particular stage in the integration of painful experiences. As the image and the style change so does the individual, who discovers previously untapped sources of creativity and inner strength.

Incorporating clinical examples with theoretical insight taken from Freud, Jung, Balint, Milner, Winnicott and others the author describes the different ways patients experience art therapy and the shifting role of the therapist responding to their needs.

'When working as an art therapist . . . I am cut off from my creative activity and can only observe the patient at work. I try to follow an experience that is rooted in the unconscious impulses which shape the work: the beginning, when the patient moves to sit or stand before a chosen art material and alters it in some way, through handling of the paint or clay; what is obliterated and what is preserved of the preliminary marks; and the patient's response to his finished work . . . it is this silent dialogue with the art material and the changing emotions that accompany it that is as much if not more important than the final object.'

R.M. Simon has developed her technique over more than 50 years working as an art therapist with children and adults, individuals and groups.

I am trying to talk about a state of mind that does in a
sense stop being that state of mind as soon as we separate
ourself from it sufficiently to talk about it in logical terms.
(Milner, *The Suppressed Madness of Sane Men*)

Symbolic Images in Art
As Therapy

R.M. Simon

London and New York

First published 1997
by Routledge
11 New Fetter Lane, London EC4P 4EE

Simultaneously published in the USA and Canada
by Routledge
29 West 35th Street, New York, NY 10001

©1996 R.M. Simon

Typeset in Times Ten by Florencetype Ltd, Stoodleigh, Devon

Printed and bound in Great Britain by
Butler & Tanner, London and Frome

British Library Cataloguing in Publication Data
A catalogue record for this book is available from the British Library

Library of Congress Cataloguing in Publication Data
Simon, R.M. (Rita M.)
   Symbolic images in art as therapy / R.M. Simon.
      p.   cm.
   Includes bibliographical references and index
   1. Art therapy   I. Title.
RC489.A7S558 1996
616.89'1656–dc20   95–39590

ISBN   0–415–12227–9 (hbk)
            0–415–12228–7 (pbk)

Contents

ERRATUM

In the plate section following page 118, Plates 2 and 3 have been transposed in relation to their captions.

Figures

Plates

Acknowledgements

I would like to record my gratitude to all who have enabled me to write this book; first of all the patients who have shared so much of their inner and outer lives with me through their art – who taught me that we all need art in order to share ourselves.

Then I wish I could express my gratitude to those who continue to feed my understanding: to William Blake, Michael Balint, Sigmund Freud, Marion Milner and Donald Winnicott, whose writings help me to express and clarify my ideas.

Nor do I forget the good fortune that introduced me to Dr Lovel Barnes, Dr Joshua Bierer and Dr Eric Strauss, who first brought me to appreciate in myself and others the need to create symbolic images when we cannot find them ready-made.

Finally, my thanks to Edwina Welham and the publishers for their generous support for this work.

A NOTE ON THE TEXT

Pseudonyms have been used throughout when discussing patients, and all other means of identification have been disguised.

A NOTE ON THE ILLUSTRATIONS

All artwork by patients appearing in this and my previous book, *The Symbolism of Style*, is in the Rita Simon Collection at the Wellcome Institute Library, London.

Figure 2.12 is a reproduction of an untitled sketch by William Roberts, copyright the estate of the artist.

Introduction

I understand creative initiative to be an instinctive response to mental conflict, and creative art to be a symbolic container for unassimilated experiences. Professional artists seek to resolve unfamiliar or conflicting experiences through the images they create, although the effort of creating a containing form may prove extremely stressful.

When creative initiative is blocked, an adult or child feels helpless and, if this enforced passivity is unrelieved, there is a real danger of mental or physical illness. If this occurs, an art therapist can provide the conditions in which creative life can be resumed.

If we are to describe art therapy in any depth we try to translate non-verbal material into common language, but a translation necessarily lacks many associations that are implied in the original. The inferences, analogies and allusions that form poetic language are the fabric of all creative art and, although the subject matter of a piece of writing, a picture or a sculpture might be simple or mundane, it is symbolic, containing a deeper meaning that is implied by the way the image is created.

It is the original form of a work that distinguishes it from work that is not art; the symbolic image provides a form that takes us beyond the literal meaning of its subject, but symbolic imagery cannot be created by conscious design and therefore evades complete description. The difficulty of doing justice to symbolic imagery has engaged me throughout this and my previous book.

Before art was recognized as a therapeutic procedure, I, as an artist, without thinking about it simply assumed that creative art was the medium for unassimilated experiences. Art was creative just because it does create a way of assimilating meanings that would be incomprehensible otherwise. Although these experiences were not necessarily the things that consciously troubled me, they inevitably blocked my mental freedom to be creative and to appreciate the creative work of some others until they had been given form. Although I might start to work with a conscious idea of what I was going to do, at some point my work developed its own logic, a logic that it forced me to follow. This experience is common to artists and gives them a sense of authority towards their work, as if at some point it reaches an extraordinary moment, when it seems as if 'the work takes over'. The artist's momentary passivity implies a willing surrender of conscious will.

I imagined that this experience was peculiar to artists, whose 'genius was akin to madness'. Consequently, I was surprised to see that some non-artists could be freely creative in this way when, during the Second World War, I was asked to open my studio to a small group of patients from a psychiatric hospital.

These people obviously valued an opportunity to draw, paint and use clay. They did not want to be taught anything. They worked intensely and sometimes found it difficult to stop, but they differed from artists in an important way; they did not value their finished work and rarely took it away with them or even looked at it again.

Later, when art therapy came under psychiatric consideration, I found that the doctors were interested in art products but had no experience of creating art or observing it being made. Thus, the integrated experience of art as 'process in product' was split, with psychotherapy entering the gap made between the two.

When working as an art therapist I experience this split, for I am cut off from creative activity and can only observe the patient at work. I try to follow an experience that is rooted in unconscious impulses that shape the work, from the beginning, when the patient moves to sit or stand before a chosen art material and alters it in some way, through the handling of the paint or clay – what is obliterated and what is preserved of the preliminary marks – to the patient's response to his finished work.

The clues are easy to miss, especially when I am working with a group; yet it is this silent dialogue with the art material and the changing emotions that accompany it that are equally, if not more important than the final object. For example, there was an occasion I remember from my first group. A woman came, looking deeply disturbed and angry, saying that she would spit. I did not want her to spit in my studio, so I handed her some paper as a place for her spit on and then she scribbled on it with grey chalk. As she continued to smear and dab the paper, lines began to form a blurred, greyish picture of a curtained window with the face of a crying child staring out of it. The smeared lines and dots faintly resembled rain. Nothing was said but as she dragged lines and smeared dots on the drawing, she wept.

This anecdote is quickly told, but the activity itself progressed over the time that was needed to realize her change of mood. The way the chalk was handled, the extent to which she reached out from her crouched position to make some horizontal strokes and later used these lines to form a window-frame for the circle of the child's face, all contributed to a release of her tension, all contributed to the symbolic container for her feelings. Although, at the time, the therapeutic process was beyond words, the experience of creating out of destructive feelings was an important part of her recovery.

Michael Balint writes of the difficulty in describing certain types of patient who express their unconscious thoughts as pictures, images or sounds which:

> may without much ado change their meaning or merge into each other – as they do, in fact, in dreams.

> (Balint 1986: 97)

In the following chapters I have tried to give an account of the processes and products of art therapy with adults and children in a number of different situations. I am grateful to the publisher who has generously allowed me to reproduce so many of the works. To discuss the way I have understood them I have had to invent some words and borrow others and still the reader will have to fill in some unavoidable gaps. The book is a companion volume to *The Symbolism of Style* (Simon 1991) but I also intend it to stand alone. For this reason I have included a brief review of the theory of art styles in the first chapter, before moving on to present particular examples of my work with adults and children.

REFERENCES

Balint, M. (1986) *The Basic Fault*, London: Tavistock.
Milner, M. (1987) *The Suppressed Madness of Sane Men*, London and New York: Tavistock.
Simon, R. M. (1991) *The Symbolism of Style*, London: Routledge.

Chapter 1

The Circle in the Square

Although babies cannot draw pictures I think they are capable [except through lack of skill] of depicting themselves by a circle at certain moments of their first months. Perhaps if all is going well they can achieve this soon after birth, at any rate we have good evidence that at six months a baby is at times using the circle or sphere as a diagram of self.

(Winnicott 1978: 253)

In this chapter I shall outline the importance of art styles in understanding the conflict faced by an adult or child who comes for art therapy. I describe this conflict as the intolerable stress of unassimilated experience that has paralysed creative initiative.

Creative art is symbolic, leading us beyond simple representation to the symbolism of its style. A tree can be painted or drawn in a number of different ways, and the one that presents the completed work reflects the artist's use of the tree. The image may be recollected or based on sight, yet it will contain the artist's attitude, whether this was a conscious intention or not. When a style is unvarying, we can say that it symbolizes the artist's attitude to life.

We recognize the language of art immediately in the lines, forms, colours and tones that shape the subject-matter. In these elements our eyes comprehend implications that would need many words to explain; although some of the things we perceive can scarcely be put into words, they may be the most important part of our experiences.

THE SUBJECT IN CREATIVE ART

Over the last fifty years I have seen creative art recognized as a form of therapy for adults and children suffering from exceptional levels of stress. The justification for viewing art as therapeutic cannot be based upon any proven facts, since so much happens below the level of consciousness. However, my experience over time has led me to recognize certain consistent factors that we know as styles of presentation. If I am to be of help to a troubled adult or child, I need to be particularly sensitive to non-verbal communications: I must feel my way intuitively, learning whether I help best by words or by actions, such as a gesture or the expression on my face. Even when an interpretation is asked for, these difficulties remain. There are times when words are very helpful in confirming an emerging insight, enabling the patient to distance him- or herself from the work.

If I talk about art with a patient we inevitably objectify it; a painting or a sculpture becomes visible to us both but this is not necessarily therapeutic: the patient may still intimately identify with the creative process, and a premature 'sharing' could be painfully intrusive, forcing a defence manoeuvre by agreeing or disagreeing with the comments I offer.

I need constantly to be aware that verbal communication can be the patient's way of relinquishing all responsibility for the object. I need to look behind the apparent image, the subject or anecdote, to the symbolic language of its style of presentation if I am to understand the way in which a troubled adult or child is unconsciously moving towards the resolution of conflict.

SYMBOLISM IN CHILD ART

The whole range of art styles can be seen in the drawings and paintings of growing children, developing from the time they first interest themselves in the marks that occur through thoughtless scribbles with a loaded brush or pen. Soon after their first year of life, young children actively enjoy putting down strokes or scribbled masses of colour that may be spaced separately or painted over each other. Soon they pay particular attention to any Circles that appear accidentally or from the circular movements of the brush. Little children of about sixteen months will laboriously join curved lines to complete a Circle.

The Circle

I have come to understand the Circle as a symbol of the Self as an entity. Little children show great persistence in making Circles and, having mastered this, they soon need to embellish them in some way. Embellishments may be added within the Circle's circumference, or lines may break through the Circle to link inside with outside. Sooner or later there is a further development, when the Circle is enclosed within a Square.

In Plates 1, 2 and 3, the child first paints with strokes of yellow that form a solid mass; then she changes to green and paints a circular line overlapping the yellow mass. The point of juncture is overworked and

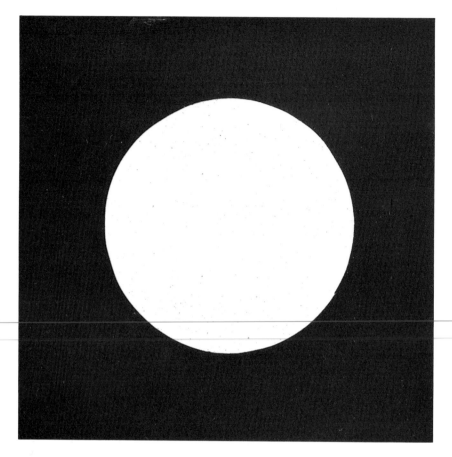

Figure 1.1 The Circle in the Square

becomes another mass. Finally, the child's face shows her pleasure as she overpaints the green Circle until it is solid, with two areas extending to contact the edge of the containing paper.

The Square

The original shape of the area surrounding the Circle is the surface on which it is created, but if this is very large, like a wall, for instance, a Square is drawn round the Circle. This composite image symbolizes the sense of Self in relation to all that is not the Self.

The Circle in the Square is our earliest image of integration, our need to be ourselves as separate from and also part of life (Figure 1.1).

Elaborations of the Circle in the Square

When a little child needs to distinguish him- or herself from others he or she will draw a symbolic Circle in a Square. If drawing materials are not available these shapes may be projected upon the environment. For instance, a Circle made by a wet cup on a check tablecloth may be studied in strict relation to the cloth pattern or its creases; a pattern or motif on a flowery wallpaper may be scribbled over to isolate an accidental combination of shapes that conform to the symbolic image of a Circle or a Square. Extra lines or colours also signify the Circle as a face, for instance, or the Square as a house.

Archaic art is epitomized in the drawings of young children; it is large in scale, simple and formal, ignoring natural appearances and facts or using them quite arbitrarily. However, as children approach puberty Archaic formality is given up and the work becomes more detailed, specific or naturalistic. The emphasis shifts from the dominance of subjective experience to a more objective view of life.

In symbolic terms, the Circle is increasingly invaded by the contents of the Square until the boundary line fades from view. Children who cannot make this change will continue as primitive artists or give up pictorial art altogether.

ADULT ART STYLES

Archaic art is obviously different from Traditional art in ways that are reflected in children's developing art styles, but the difference is more apparent than real. Although the symbolic image of Circle in Square may be totally obscured when a work of art depicts images of external reality, it continues as the organization of the picture in ways we describe as the pictorial composition.

Linear and Massive styles

Both the Archaic and the Traditional style can be created by outlines that give an effect of flatness to the shapes. The Linear emphasis in Archaic art contributes a great deal to an effect of remoteness from the material world: outline is used in Traditional art to separate details clearly from one another. Both Archaic and Traditional art use mass as colour or tone that gives an effect of solid weight to the images; in Archaic art the mass seems protrusive, extending towards the spectator, while in Traditional art the forms appear to recede into the distance. All these differences can be contained within four basic styles – Archaic Linear and Massive art and Traditional Linear and Massive art.

Postures and gestures creating art

A style does not materialize like an instant photograph; it is an image created by the posture and gestures of the adult or child who makes it. Archaic Linear art is primarily an instinctive response to the sensuous pleasure of the physical activity of engaging the whole body in large sweeping movements of hand and arm. The artist's poise allows a large circle or a straight line to appear (Figure 1.2).

Figure 1.2 Archaic Linear, typical posture and gesture

If the creative impulse becomes exciting, the actions may become overdetermined, florid or perseverative, with paint or scribble overworked until the shape transcends its boundary line and gives the illusion of standing proud of the pictorial surface. This is the Massive form of Archaic art (Figure 1.3).

Figure 1.3 Archaic Massive, typical posture and gesture

Traditional art also has a Massive style but this is created in almost the opposite way. Instead of the wild delight of violent contrasts of brilliant colour in massive areas of paint, there is everywhere the quiet restraint of subtle tones and cool colours that blend together in delicate brush strokes to form illusions of space and light. These are the gestures that create Traditional Massive art (Figure 1.4).

Figure 1.4 Traditional Massive, typical posture and gesture

The other Traditional style is Linear, dominated by a need for clarity, to distinguish each thing from the others. Shapes are separated by lines or abrupt changes of colour or tone that affirm their separate boundaries. This work looks, and often is, obsessional, being carefully planned and drawn, using small movements of the fingers with the wrist supported by the pictorial surface. The tense, crouched position that is typical of this style cannot sustain a long straight line or a large Circle without mechanical aid (Figure 1.5).

TRANSITIONAL STYLES

Although the Archaic and Traditional styles are quite distinct, most paintings contain some elements of more than one style. The two Massive styles can blend, linking Archaic to Traditional art and the two Linear styles act in the same way, allowing a style to change smoothly from Linear to Massive, or Traditional to Archaic. If these transitional styles contain equal quantities of the two adjacent styles they will show some characteristic features of each.

The Archaic styles are loosely linked by a diagonal emphasis that disrupts the large symmetrical shapes based on the Circle, while the Linear transition fragments the composition with details that are complete, but separate, strongly outlined or spaced apart, stereotyped or replaced by hieroglyphics. Further movement round the Circle of Styles may be

Figure 1.5 Archaic Linear, typical posture and gesture

towards Archaic Linear art but, if this is blocked, the artist or patient, adult or child, can turn their creative initiative to words, dictating stories or poems with the authoritative force that they brought to their visual art.

When the Massive styles are in transition, the effect of naturalistic space is disturbed, with things intended to be distant being placed towards the top of the picture while those intended to be near are placed on a horizontal line at the bottom, indicating a foreground. The work often looks clumsy, overloading the available space.

If the two Traditional art styles overlap, naturalism suffers from conceptual determinants that emphasize certain shapes or colours that have literal associations.

THE CIRCLE OF STYLES

As a result of my discovery of these transitions between the basic styles I was able to arrange all eight styles as a continuous circle (Figure 1.6), allowing for change from one attitude to another. Change can follow the clockwise or the anti-clockwise direction. Although my diagram places the Archaic Linear style at the top, the Circle of Styles may be entered at any point.

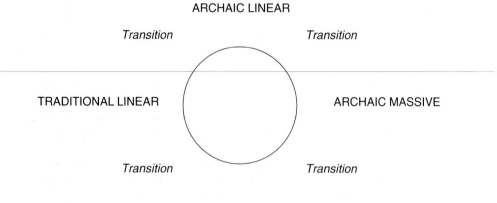

Figure 1.6 The Circle of Styles

We can see changes of style in two ways; there are the immediate changes that occur during a creation of a single piece of work such as I described earlier, which might be temporary or permanent; and there are continuous, minimal changes that continue during the whole course of the art therapy commitment. The changes I refer to are not accidental; nor can they be contrived, but rather they are generated by our instinctive need to symbolize our relation to life as both the same and different from others, lasting as long as life itself.

STYLES AS ATTITUDES OF MIND

I will use the art of painting as my example, but a similar thing occurs in any plastic material that tends first to be marked with fingerprints or flattened and incised and then, in the massive stage worked on as a solid object, to be moulded as a three-dimensional form. In the basic Archaic shapes we have a whole vocabulary of expressive images that reflect the dominance of sensuous and emotional life.

The sensuous life dominates the first few years. This 'body ego', as Freud called it, contains the sense of Self as immediate experience symbolized by the Circle in the Square. This immediacy has the quality of hallucination in which the seer and the seen momentarily dissolve into each other – the boundary of the Circle fades. This sense of verity has no place in objective reality, but maintains its inner truth (Plate 4).

As sensuous reality becomes assailed by the intensities of emotion, the continuity of Archaic Linear shapes is shattered in parallel with the situation extensively studied by Freud under the name of the Oedipus complex. Harmony is restored and enriched in the vibrant colours and forms of the Massive style; the attributes of love and hate, sadness and joy dominate this phase of our lives and give emotional intensity to the images of Archaic art.

When an artist is affected by traditional culture, the dominance of inner reality is moderated by the outer world of perception. No longer Self-centred but projected upon mountains or forests, cows, or factories, the boundary of the Circle lightens or dissolves as the artist's identification with the objects perceived or recollected enables him or her to create the illusion of appearances.

This Traditional Massive style gives the artist's intuition full rein and he or she need not be concerned with facts unless they become insistent. Some artists make the transition from one Traditional style to the other by introducing a few conceptual 'markers' into their naturalistic work; certain parts are emphasized – the blue of the Virgin's robe does not fade into space as do other parts of a painting, but as we move further around the Circle of Styles we see perceptions modified increasingly in conceptual arts. First, the diffusion of space and light is disrupted by local colours and shapes of ideas and ideals, then factual representation further interrupts the unity of the painting and intrudes upon the artist's sense of integrated being. Ideas may seem to be the only means by which the individual can survive if the Self-Circle is fragmented by the area of the Square.

ART AS THERAPY

Regardless of age, cultural background or psychiatric diagnosis, and only partially affected by a physical condition, adult and child patients show a variety of art styles in their work that symbolize the various attitudes they hold towards life. Some will exert dexterous control of a medium and will display the level of representational skill that is generally expected of adult art but others will express themselves in fluent, simple shapes that may be abstract or developed with simple attributes (Simon 1991: 104–6).

I cannot say that visual expression in art is the only requirement for art to be therapeutic. The holding situation of the setting is not only the paint and paper: the art therapist is needed to ensure privacy and concerned attention to the patient's needs – needs for both freedom and containment, for both silence and speech, for the two aspects of art (its symbolic meaning and its value as an object) to be visible to the art therapist as well as to its creator.

SUMMARY

The subject of a painting or sculpture is so immediately attractive that the style of the image tends to be overlooked unless it startles the viewer. Nevertheless, art as a therapy depends as much on the way that a work of art is created as on the subject that is depicted.

Eight art styles are postulated, presenting various elaborations of the first, basic shape of a Circle in a Square. Apparently, we have an instinctive need to create this configuration as a verification of its symbolic significance.

This chapter offers a condensed version of the theory that is fully described in my previous book (Simon 1991).

REFERENCES

Balint, M. (1986) *The Basic Fault*, London: Tavistock.
Simon, R. M. (1991) *The Symbolism of Style*, London: Routledge.
Winnicott, D. W. (1978) *Through Paediatrics to Psychoanalysis*, London: Hogarth.

Chapter 2

Mr Pauli, madly serious play

I begin this study with a very old-fashioned joke:

> One day, a gentleman met a naked madman, standing all alone, wearing a hat. The gentleman said 'My good man, why are you standing about without any clothes?' The madman replied, 'Nobody comes to see me.' The gentleman was not entirely satisfied. He said, 'I can understand that, but why are you wearing a hat?' The madman then replied, 'Somebody might.'

I use this joke for a number of reasons; first because it does not 'add up' or offer a logical solution. It speaks to me about my experience, that there is never the perfect communication between individuals that we want to find, particularly when the individuals are called therapist (gentleman) and patient (madman). These gaps in ordinary communication were very clear in my contact with Mr Pauli, but my experience with him also showed me that even the slightest contact can be useful.

The joke shows our assumptions about madness, our ignorance of other ways of thinking that Blake explored in his poem *Mental Traveller* (Blake 1939: 325). Madness was a man who stands naked, wearing a hat for, in the days when this joke was funny, it was mad for a man to wear a hat and go naked. Nowadays, on a hot beach the reverse could be true. The joke is on the gentleman therapist who expects a rational answer and gets one that seems irrational.

MR PAULI

I met the man I shall call Mr Pauli in 1941, before art was generally recognized as therapeutic. He was referred by his psychiatrist to a small art group I held as a sort of 'drop-in' facility for any patient who wished to paint or draw on a Sunday afternoon. In those days I was looking for aesthetic values, whether the art was by patients or by anyone else. I assumed that all art had therapeutic value and if the art work was aesthetically

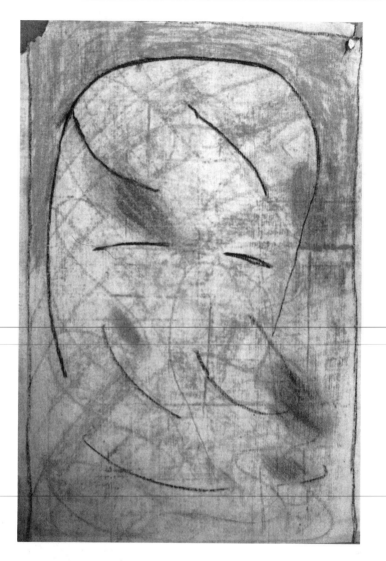

Figure 2.1 Archaic transition

satisfying then the artist's mental health must be beyond question. I would also have said that there was a bad art, art that was sick.

In this art group I did not try to teach; I was not a teacher but I would answer simple questions about such practical matters as mixing colours or mounting finished work. I was surprised to see that people who came regularly became deeply absorbed in imaginative work, and the only intervention I made was to introduce a group doodle as a means of bringing each session to a close. Painting under these conditions seemed good enough for most people, who came to communicate through their art work. Mr Pauli was such a person: very quiet, and non-committal.

Mr Pauli made twelve drawings that I appreciated as art. Now I see in these drawings a therapeutic progress. I will try to describe how I responded to them at the time and also my ideas about them now. On

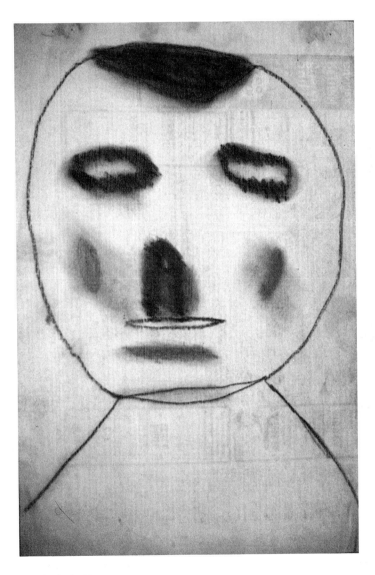

Figure 2.2 Archaic Linear

his first visit Mr Pauli did no more than make a few faint marks with coloured chalks on paper, but when I invited him to put this 'doodle' on an easel and look to see what he might make of it, he put it up and eventually thought that it looked like a face. With some encouragement he added a few black strokes to delineate the face and added a block of pale green to outline the top of the head (Figure 2.1).

The next week he returned and his drawing surprised me by its assurance (Figure 2.2). He drew a circle about 12 inches in circumference and worked determinedly to make it into a face much bigger than his own, spending most of the hour doggedly outlining the features. In the end he seemed shocked when someone in the group treated it as a joke and said that he had drawn a portrait of Hitler. After this offence he did not come to the group again.

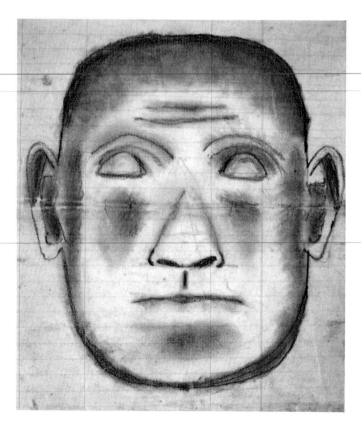

Figure 2.3 Archaic Massive

MR PAULI BY HIMSELF

Some time after this, Mr Pauli turned up unexpectedly on my doorstep and handed me a drawing. I was pleased and surprised that he was still interested in art and encouraged him to return. He continued to bring drawings now and again for many months, handing them to me at the door without comment and walking off immediately. Perhaps this behaviour seems a bit odd, but as I had no idea what to expect from psychiatric patients I felt satisfied that he was using art in his own way.

He was middle-aged and I knew nothing about him except that he had been a 'chronic' patient, worn down by years of mental illness that had isolated him from his family and friends. After being discharged from hospital he had taken lodgings in the then much-bombarded East End of London, where psychiatric aftercare was virtually non-existent.

Mr Pauli brought drawings at something like monthly intervals, turning up unexpectedly with a picture in a paper bag. I kept them in a folder

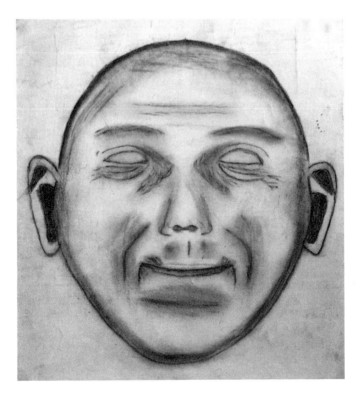

Figure 2.4 Archaic Massive

with the two he had made in the group. They were given in the sequence indicated here, but I do not know if these were all that he made.

The first three pictures use lines and masses as flat, two-dimensional images, showing obvious difficulties in presentation; the second drawing could not manage to show a nose and he failed to complete the third (Figure 2.14), which I assumed to be an attempt to imitate a photograph. I told him firmly that artists do not copy. When he turned up again with another piece of work I was delighted to see that his creative initiative had been blocked only temporarily but, when I tried to explain to him that the original artist in him had refused to collaborate with the hope of imitating art, he smiled briefly and backed down the steps.

The eyes in the first drawings (Figures 2.3 and 2.4) are blank and this made them look closed or blind; I had assumed this was an intentional feature of his art and consequently it was quite a shock to see a rather naturalistic face, with wide-open eyes in his sixth drawing (Figure 2.5), a face that looked like someone who was attending, although the mouth

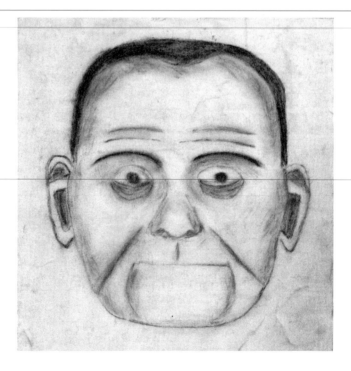

Figure 2.5 Massive transition

was too tightly shut for conversation. The face could almost be of a man in the street and, in my ignorance, I thought that Mr Pauli was now ready to face the world as an artist.

During our brief encounters on my doorstep I tried to encourage him to look at painting and sculpture; I mounted the drawing like a picture, but when I offered to show it to him the next time he came, he ignored me. He was following another line altogether, for the next drawings returned to the simplicity of his previous style with the addition of colour; the eyes remained open with an intense stare. The drawing shown here as Figure 2.6 has the look of someone facing something that demands moral or physical strength.

Figure 2.6 Archaic Massive

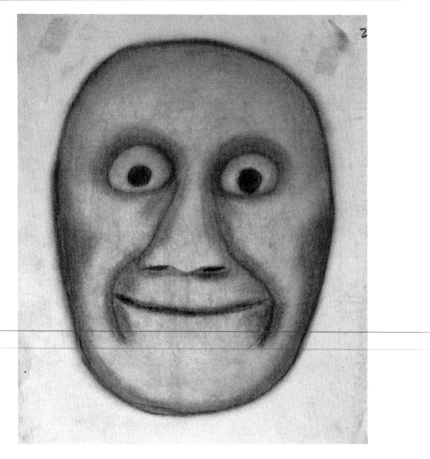

Figure 2.7 Archaic Massive

I was fascinated by the effect of awakened energy in these drawings and looked forward to the next (Figure 2.7), which again surprised me by its happy, even delighted smile and the naturalistic colour/tone of the face.

The next work (Figure 2.8) in charcoal and red chalk looked passionately, frantically eager; the dark tones of the mask seemed to push it forward beyond the white paper of its background and this intensity was continued in the next drawing (Figure 2.9) in another, even more startling development and modification of his art style. The mask-like convention of an oval disc had been modified to the shape of a head, temples and jaw, with the nose drawn as if tensely projecting from the face. I felt I was looking at the tragic mask of Pagliacci, the universal clown, and I felt the emotion whitening its nose like pressure on my own nasal bone.

Figure 2.8 Archaic Massive

I had come to feel rather protective towards this silent man; it was all very well, I thought, for me to delight in these drawings as works of art, but suppose they seemed to Mr Pauli, alone in his room, to be visitations of the devil that should be fought or destroyed? Why would he not join the companionship of artists? Suppose he wondered, I thought, whether his art was making him go mad?

Although the pain expressed in this last drawing troubled me, I did not know how to talk to him about it when he stood poised for flight on my doorstep; but after he had gone I decided that I must say something to give his work its frame of art.

When next he came I insisted on talking for a few minutes about the place of art in the world, adding that his art style reminded me of African dance masks, Sumerian art and and the art of Archaic Greece and Rome. I think that I also mentioned ancient Chinese and Javanese art, trying to widen his view beyond the traditional naturalism that I

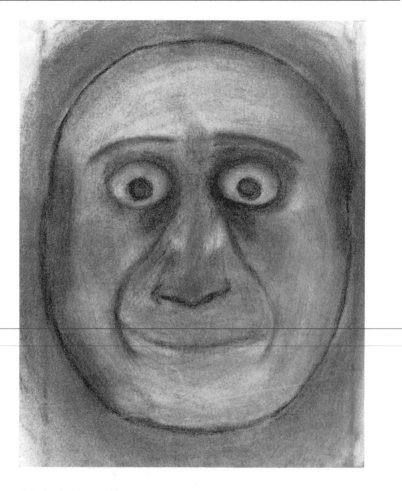

Figure 2.9 Archaic transition

thought was probably his idea of what art should be. Mr Pauli edged away, silent as usual, vaguely smiling and, apparently, not attending to this rigmarole at all.

It was some time before he brought another drawing (Figure 2.10), another disembodied face; this one had a rueful look, sad and humorous, coloured lightly in pink and green. The face seemed to emerge from the background or perhaps to be submerged in it.

Mr Pauli brought only one more piece of work, a pencil drawing. It was a self-portrait from sight, showing delicacy of execution combined with factual observation (Figure 2.11). The head was turned to the sophisticated three-quarter position beloved of Renaissance artists, and I felt I

Figure 2.10 Massive transition

was looking at a drawing by a student of Holbein or William Roberts. Every drawing he had given me had been a surprise, but this one underlined my fears for his originality as an Archaic artist. It looked as if Mr Pauli had closed the door on his creative initiative and joined the ranks of the traditionalists. I was very sorry, and not surprised, that he did not come again.

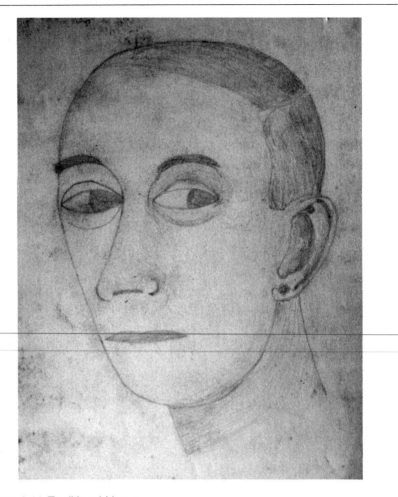

Figure 2.11 Traditional Linear

RE-EVALUATIONS

Aesthetic and therapeutic values may conflict, for we can hardly remain influenced by the sensuous and emotional effects of an art work while at the same time trying to interpret the unconscious meaning it has for us and for the individual who created it.

In my continuing attempts to understand as much as I can about art as therapy, as distinct from other forms of psychotherapy, I look back to Mr Pauli, his art and his use of me as someone who accepted his drawings without the therapeutic provision of a containing place and time or the support I could represent as an artist. I find it helpful to think about the difference between the way I saw his work then, and how I see it now.

I had responded to Mr Pauli's work aesthetically, as being true to an 'artistic' compulsion to uncover inner images evoked by an incoherent doodle, but I never knew any more about the way he made his drawings, whether he made others that he did not bring, or whether the drawings were made in the order he gave them to me. He only once spoke as he handed one to me, mentioning that he had been to the part of the National Gallery that remained open at that time and had spoken to some people there about art. The only other communication with him came ten years after; when he heard that I was leaving England he wrote briefly to wish me well. I replied, but he did not keep in touch.

Apart from my knowledge that he had been described as 'mentally ill', the sameness and difference between Mr Pauli and the madman in the joke bothered me. The madman was lonely, so was Mr Pauli; the gentleman was stupid, and had I not been equally stupid in thinking that a mental patient was an artist? The gentleman thought that he recognized a madman and I thought I recognized an artist, perhaps because I was then studying art under William Roberts and greatly admired the Massive simplification of his life drawings (Figure 2.12). Mr Pauli's untutored drawings seemed to have a similar style of simple mass that also delighted me in Sumerian art (Figure 2.13) and I wondered what Mr Pauli thought about my enthusiasm. It seemed as if he guarded his art from any sort of evaluation while needing someone only to receive what he had done. I did not know that Jung had written authoritatively about the difference between professional art and art as therapy (Jung 1972: 220) or that Michael Balint was concerned with this quality of separateness as the area of creativity (Balint 1986).

Perhaps there is a touch of truth in the notion of art being akin to madness, for art expresses things we feel but cannot rationally explain. Hanna Segal has written clearly about the difference between creativity and delusion:

> Freud emphasizes that the artist returns to reality. I think the artist never quite leaves reality. To begin with, he has an acute awareness of his internal realities. The inner reality he seeks to express, but the grasp of reality always goes with the ability to differentiate between creativity and delusion. The artist must have an outstanding reality perception of the potential and of the limitations of his material.
>
> (Segal 1991: 96)

Mr Pauli's sequence of drawings can be seen as a realization of a delusion, for it transformed his fantasy into the reality of a work of art through his perception of the potential and the limitations of the art material. Perhaps the same thing could be said of all creative art; the drawing by William Roberts starts from the actual and outer reality of the living model in space and light and abstracts from all this an illusion of weight and

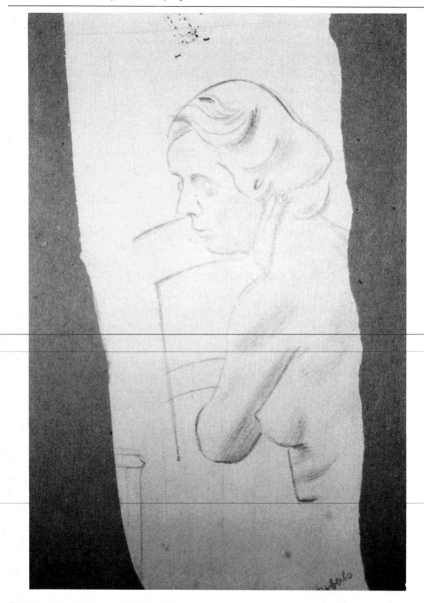

Figure 2.12 Nude by William Roberts

solid form, linking his drawing with Mr Pauli's and with the Sumerian sculpture of Figure 2.13.

The creative artist cannot tolerate confinement, either in the perceived or the remembered. Any such experiences will be used – they are the artist's material, as the paint or clay, as my young son realized when he responded irritably to a question about his art at school: 'If I could've said it I wouldn't ever have done it.'

When we suppose that we know good art from bad it is a subjective opinion, even if we happen to be an art critic, historian or art therapist. Our response to the wordless language of form, line, shape and colour depends upon our ability to recognize the object as art. For some, art is a satisfying orderliness or emotional intensity, a certain degree of formality or informality, sameness or difference from the expected. Hanna Segal sees art as an attempted reparation from the conflict arising from the depressive position (Segal 1991: 95)

These different ways of seeing art are bound to an illusory sense of their truth, and it was lucky for Mr Pauli that his way of drawing seemed truthful to me. In his first effort I saw any art student's difficulty in facing

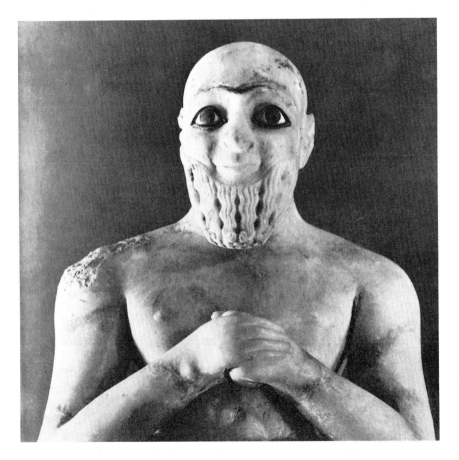

Figure 2.13 Sumerian sculpture, third millennium

a blank sheet of paper, while someone else might have seen this chaotic scribble as crazy. It was my aesthetic response to his use of the art material that I recognized; the succession of bodiless faces showed an artist's single-minded pursuit of his vision. Moreover, as an art student I had been taught to imagine myself into the object I was drawing; I had to feel myself to be the heavy pottery jug or the frail china cup – I felt that my drawing was not any good if I could not imagine being the naked model, her weight on her feet after standing still for an hour, to feel the tense muscle in my arm and calf, the balance of the bones in the spine. Consequently, I assumed that the faces Mr Pauli drew reflected how he felt them inside himself. In the assurance of his second drawing I recognized authentic Archaic art and when he developed this flat, Linear style as a solid, Massive form, his drawings had a familiar look, his art style was as familiar as a hat, set upon the naked truth of his creative impulse. Now that I can also see his work as therapeutic, I am pleased that he could work on in spite of my misguided support.

We can follow the process of Mr Pauli's recovery through the development of his art style; however, to translate a visual language into a logical sequence of words is very difficult and cumbersome. I am sorry that I must verbally carve up the aesthetic unity of his images in my need to transcribe them into words, but I am not alone in this difficulty. I am indebted to Frances Tustin for describing the same problem in writing about autistic states:

> I have called upon poets and writers to help me in this task. It seemed to me that we need to be encircled by their integrating aesthetic embrace as we go through the states of unintegration and disintegration that will be discussed.
>
> (Tustin 1986: 13)

MR PAULI'S ART STYLES

In drawing, a creative artist spontaneously selects certain aspects of reality, not so much with conscious design but in obedience to a sense of a truth that is recognized by those who share the same assumptions. Some aspects of perceived reality are selected or recalled as the art material dictates scale, shape, form and colour. I will describe Mr Pauli's drawings in this way before discussing the symbolism of his styles.

His first two drawings filled sheets of paper 12 by 18 inches. The size was a standard provision for this group; some people used the whole sheet while others only used a part. The drawings he made at home were smaller, about 9 by 12 inches.

Scale

The scale of a work of art is not its size, but the way any size is used. The drawings Mr Pauli made at home were smaller in size but equally large in scale, that is to say, that they filled the space with a single form. A huge scale suggests closeness, the position of an object as it would be if the paper were a window. In this sense, Mr Pauli's faces would be very close to the glass, some almost protruding forward as if the window was open and the face protruding. This sense of close proximity also indicates the importance of a subject, dominating everything else.

Shape

Creative art can be described as a modification of basic shapes arising from the natural movements of our limbs. We leave traces of our gestures in our paintings as we leave footsteps in the sand (Simon 1991: 58). Lines record Mr Pauli's gestures, his free movements create a complete circle and his straight lines follow a decisive gesture.

Mr Pauli's first three drawings look flat; no part seems to protrude or recede. From the blackness of the lines representing the nose (Figure 2.3) it seemed that he was aware of this limitation but was unable to visualize projection.

Form

Form is created by overworking the line or boundary of a shape, giving it an appearance of substance, of weight or organic life. This impression of volume made the mask-like faces appear as if projecting from the background.

Colour/tone

This is also a way of forming an image and, in Figures 2.9 and 2.10 green suggests a space to contain the image.

Attributes

Traditional art represents the known world of appearances and facts, but Archaic images are of the sensuous and emotional inner world that has no visible representation; its shapes, forms and colours are abstract. Symbolic images may be elaborated to indicate particular attributes, such as the blue skin of the god Krishna.

Eleven of Mr Pauli's drawings were Archaic elaborations of the basic Circle. That is to say, he created images of inner reality. Only his last drawing is truly representational, although the flesh colour of Figure 2.10 seems to anticipate the external view. Mr Pauli's visits to the National Gallery, where he was able to talk to strangers, may have contributed to this new ability to attend to external life.

A graphic representation of the styles can be helpful sometimes as a simple way of highlighting changes that may not be obvious over a long period of time.

THE SYMBOLISM OF HIS STYLES

Jung and many others have written of the use of the symbolism of the Circle in adult art. Michael Fordham, a Jungian psychotherapist interested in the symbolic Circle in child art, equated it with protective magic, completeness and a means of Self-integration (Fordham 1969: 80).

The symbolic image of the Circle seems necessary when we need to affirm our individual place in life, and we unconsciously seek it in man-made patterns and accidental arrangements. The motif is apperceived in a gesture, a vision or hallucination. Less attention has been paid to the Square as a symbol of all that is not the Self.

Frances Tustin describes the use of the Square in a drawing by a recovering autistic child, the boy John, who enlightens us about the use of these basic shapes. Tustin describes watching John making a drawing:

> The drawing turned out to be an aeroplane. He said the pointed part in front was the nose, and then he drew a thing like an eye. He drew squares, saying 'Square windows'. He does not like squares and has avoided them on most occasions. It was in keeping with his mood of today of trying to face things that he did not like.
>
> (Tustin 1990: 193)

It is interesting that John drew the Squares *inside* the containing shape of his aeroplane. As Squares symbolize things that are separate from the Self, a well child uses external reality to supply what he has not, but John was only just coming to tolerate the sharp edges of external reality, symbolized by the Square, in his own way, by incorporation.

Although laborious to describe, Mr Pauli's pictures immediately presented his relation to external reality in the varying proportions of the face, as a Circle in the Square. In the first drawing he could not find a complete Circle, only seeing a head in an hallucinatory way, as we might see a face in the moon.

At the time, I saw the second drawing as Archaic art, with the intensity of a Sumerian sculpture (Larousse 1965: 53); now I think perhaps it is an image of that archaic heritage that Freud discovered in dreams (Freud 1949: 28) and Jung named archetypes. Symbols are actually nameless, although they accommodate our ideas about meaning. I imagine that this was a reflection of his mental state and was so powerful a challenge to Mr Pauli's need of life that it roused his creative initiative to make the huge, 12-inch Circle.

The symbolism of this drawing is particularly important; in it the Circle of Self is complete, an image of wholeness that may well have been fragmented during his years of mental illness. The Circle contained attributes of his inner, sensuous life as a face that almost blocked the whole area of external reality. If this is a fair interpretation of the way he felt about himself and the image, we can imagine how shocking a careless remark about Hitler would have been.

Yet, whatever the effect of that remark, it did not stop him from trying to produce a conventional effect, based on a photograph. This drawing failed in the attempt to use his Archaic style in copying a photograph; the image rendered flat, approximating to the Square.

Once Mr Pauli had discovered emotional expression in the Archaic Massive style, he used two versions, the first smudged the outlines to give an illusion of sculptured form. This is followed by a drawing that modifies the Massive style, indicating a transition towards Traditional art.

The next three faces are full of life and colour; the Circle seems to be almost bursting with vitality but the expression in the tenth face is complex and the Circle is related to a Square of green chalk to extend beyond two boundary lines of the Square. The eleventh work seems in retreat from the Archaic inner world; the Circle is smaller and its colour/tone sinks into the background Square.

The final drawing (Figure 2.11) links the Circle of Self with the Other of his neck as a solid form. Then the mirror of his art is turned to reflect Mr Pauli from the outside, an achievement more remarkable when we consider his early attempt (Figure 2.14) to find outer reality in the copy of a photograph.

DISCUSSION

To come back to the beginning joke about the naked madman who stood alone and hoped to raise his hat to someone, Mr Pauli showed hope by coming to my art group and exhibiting the naked shape of his fragmented life; sadly, he found the incomprehension of that fictitious gentleman, but Mr Pauli's need to trust an inner reality was stronger than this discouragement.

When I looked at the sequence of his drawings I longed to know if the changes in his style instigated the therapeutic change or if the therapy was the creative impetus itself, regardless of what he did or how he did it. Freud, as so often, had already looked at the question of visual thinking:

We must not be led away, in the interests of simplification perhaps, into forgetting the importance of optical memory residues – those of *things* (as opposed to words) – or to deny that it is possible for thought-processes to become conscious though a revision to visual residues, and that in many people this seems to be a favourite method.

(Freud 1949: 23; emphasis in original)

In my present efforts to reach beyond the image to its influence on mental health I have need of a long quotation from Winnicott:

we tend to think of health in terms of ego defences. We say that it is healthy when these defences are not rigid, etc. But we seldom reach the point at which we can start to describe what life is like apart from illness or absence of illness.

That is to say we have yet to tackle the question of *what life itself is about*. Our psychotic patients force us to give attention to this

Figure 2.14 Traditional Linear

sort of basic problem. We now see that it is not instinctual satis-faction that makes a baby begin to be, to feel that life is real, to find life worth living. ... I could use Buffon's saying "Le style est l'homme même". When one speaks of a man one speaks of him ALONG WITH the summation of his cultural experiences. The whole forms a unit.

I have used the term cultural experience as an extension of the idea of transitional phenomena and of play without being certain that I can define the word culture. The accent is indeed upon experience. In using the word culture I am thinking of the inherited tradition. I am thinking of something that is in the common pool of humanity, into which indi-viduals and groups of people may contribute, and from which we may all draw *if we have somewhere to put what we find*.

(Winnicott 1971: 98–9; emphases in original)

These statements help me to see how mental health depends upon expe-riencing and being experienced: the therapeutic place of Mr Pauli's drawings and the madman's hat.

Patients need the privacy of individual art therapy if they are to recog-nize the changes that anticipate conscious insight, but these changes may not be verbalized. However, Mr Pauli was not in the studio but balancing on a step, and I now see his position as precarious. Jung emphasizes the therapeutic value of creating art. While discussing the dangers of primary emotion confined within the sensuous life of undifferentiated feeling, he writes:

To the extent that I managed to translate the emotions into images – that is to say, to find the images which were concealed in the emotions – I was inwardly calmed and reassured. If I had left these images hidden in the emotions I might have been torn to pieces by them.

(Jung 1972: 281)

Elsewhere he is emphatic about the importance of symbolic image-making, which he describes as confronting the unconscious:

The essential thing is to differentiate oneself from these unconscious contents by personifying them, and at the same time to bring them into relationship with consciousness.

(Jung 1972: 211)

Although I could not ask Mr Pauli if he found himself calmed and reas-sured by drawing, his art styles do assure me that he was less confused and introverted after he had made the drawings and given them to me over a period of time. However, they do not answer the question of rela-tion between perception and apperception. In 'There is no Natural Religion' Blake argued that:

Man's desires are limited by his perceptions;
none can desire what he has not perceived.

(Blake 1939: 3)

The psychoanalyst Michael Balint describes the need for imagery in psychoanalysis.

> As soon as an external object appears on the scene, such as a completed work of art, a mathematical or philosophical thesis, a piece of insight or understanding that can be expressed in words, or as soon as the illness reaches a stage at which the individual can complain to someone about it, an external object is there and we can get to work with our analytical methods.

(Balint 1986: 24)

I leave the final word with Balint, who, speaking of the area of creativity, describes its silences and imperviousness to psychological interpretation that call on the creative imagination and flexibility of the therapist's own creative imagination:

> The task of translating the meaning of observed phenomena into adult language – whether for scientific or therapeutic purposes – is based on the presence of an adult vocabulary and an adult grammar that exist only at the Oedipal level. As far as we know, the unconscious has no vocabulary . . . mainly pictures, images, sounds which may without much ado change their meaning or merge into each other – as they do, in fact, in dreams. It seems that, in the unconscious, words have the same vagueness of contour and colour as the images seen in a dream, a kind of grey in grey; though cathected with a great deal of fleeting emotion and affect.

(Balint 1986: 97)

> Perhaps, if we can change our own approach from that of considering the silence as a symptom of resistance, to studying it as a possible area of information, we may learn something about this area of the mind.

(Balint 1986: 27)

SUMMARY

This chapter offers an example of drawing as a means of self-therapy, organized by a patient who can only use art therapy in a minimal way. Mr Pauli discovered an impulse to draw after twice attending a free art group, then he continued to make drawings at home. The images he created symbolize the different stages of his recovery. Only the patient could heal himself, but to do this he needed to find a place where his discoveries would be appreciated. Mr Pauli chose my doorstep.

REFERENCES

Balint, M. (1986) *The Basic Fault*, London: Tavistock.
Blake, W. (1939) *Poems and Prophecies*, London: J.M. Dent & Sons Ltd.
Fordham, M. (1969) *Children as Individuals*, London: Hodder & Stoughton.
Freud, S. (1946) 'The Moses of Michelangelo', in *Collected Papers*.
—— (1949) *An Outline of Psycho-analysis*, London: Hogarth Press.
Jung, C. G. (1972) *Memories, Dreams, Reflections*, London: Fontana.
Larousse World Mythology (1965), London: Paul Hamlyn.
Segal, H. (1991) *Dream, Phantasy and Art*, London: Routledge.
Simon, R. M. (1991) *The Symbolism of Style*, London: Routledge.
Tustin, F. (1986) *Autistic Barriers in Neurotic Patients*, London: Karnac Books.
—— (1990) *The Protective Shell in Adults and Children*, London: Karnac Books.
Winnicott, D. W. (1971) *Playing and Reality*, London: Tavistock.

Chapter 3

Kitchen Art

he [the artist] is not the only one who has a life of phantasy; the intermediate world of phantasy is sanctioned by general human consent,
and every hungry soul looks to it for comfort and consolation.

(Freud 1961: 314)

Kitchen Art is the name given to a provision for small groups of adults
and children to share a common interest in free painting, writing and
playing with clay. I shall describe its place in art therapy by first giving a
practical example.

JEFF

Jeff was an old country man who had never gone to school or worked for
his living. When I met him he looked rather dishevelled, with a vacant grin
that served to acknowledge, if not answer, anything that was said to him.
He lived with his family and appeared to occupy himself by walking about
his village for most of the day. His neighbours referred to him as 'the boy'.

When invited to a Kitchen Art group he chose paint and immediately
made a surprising picture (Figure 3.1), choosing a large piece of paper
that he painted in the Archaic Linear style, carefully mixing the colours
to get the tints he needed. In all this he showed a serious and decisive
manner that his acquaintances had not seen before.

The first three pictures were of the same subject, huge, symmetrical
paintings with a central motif, rather like a tree or an idol, surrounded
by objects like votive offerings. Quite soon after this, Jeff began to overpaint the edges of the flat areas with a darker tone, giving an effect of
solidity to the shapes (Figure 3.2).

Jeff was not asked about his pictures, nor did he talk about them,
although he was pleased to see them admired. Each week he began a fresh
painting, carefully mixing the paints until they satisfied his sense of colour
harmony. Each painting had a harmonious tonal range: in paintings that
were light in tone he added a tint of colour to white paint, in an almost
professional way, rather than starting with a colour and then lightening it.

Figure 3.1 Jeff's first painting, Archaic Linear

Figure 3.2 Jeff's later painting, Archaic Massive

Although it was obvious that painting was important to him, he did not always finish his picture or want to keep it, or even refer to it again. He attended every session and during this time he seemed quietly self-satisfied and less socially inept.

This is not a dramatic story of healing but of the unobtrusive acquisition of a man's self-respect. It might be difficult for a psychotherapeutically orientated reader to distinguish Kitchen Art from a social club where helpful and friendly overtures are made to a disadvantaged member. I will try to describe what is different about a Kitchen Art group.

Jeff's story does not make a dramatic one but I offer it as a simple example of the place of creative initiative in respect and self-respect. The same response is seen when a patient with 'senile dementia' paints a landscape or writes a story that reveals the individual within the patient to family, medical and nursing staff in a geriatric ward.

A kitchen is not a club, a studio or a recreation room: the group is family-sized and, like a family round the kitchen table, members share a common interest. Children may join in, no one has to be sociable – there is time to use a simple art material and to have tea and a biscuit.

Kitchen Art has an educational value that has nothing to do with learning a technique. The learning process occurs through the participants' discovery of their own untapped responses to inner and outer life. For some people a response will take the form of the unintentioned appearance of space and light in a smudge of paint that transforms it into a landscape (Figure 3.3) or the elegant pattern left by the cutting wire in a piece of clay. For others it will be awakened trust in moments of abstraction, when the mind is not in charge of the hand and 'anything' is allowed to be painted or modelled. It might be listening to the inner ear when a few words form themselves into a chant unbidden, to become a poem demanding to be written down before it slips away.

The mother who paints beside her exhausting toddler can appreciate his art through empathetic understanding of the physical and imaginative process of creating her own drawing. Neighbours who only pass the time of day in the street can share the unspoken intimacy of creative work when they paint together in a kitchen. The Archaic art of very old people can be appreciated by those who enjoy children's art, and the slow learner like Jeff, who suffers from an inability to take knowledge from others, can tap his inner knowledge when it becomes visible through colour, shape or form.

Creative art could be seen as a secret weapon against prejudice and fear of strangeness when the artist's own pre-judging of his or her art is in abeyance and the imagination is allowed to reveal a strange new world. The rationale of 'art' protects fantasy from being taken for real – 'it is only a story', says the rational mind when irrational imagination speaks truly about our inner life.

Figure 3.3 The Seaside, Traditional Massive

TWO REALITIES

From birth, the inner reality of our needs must be modified by the limitations of our circumstances. This painful dilemma gives rise to wishes that hope for eventual fulfilment. In creative art these wishes find expression and the sort of resolution that Freud considered to be a sublimation. Wishes and hopes are given a form that is real in the sense that it creates a real object, painting, claywork or poem visible to anyone, yet unreal in the sense that it has no independent life. The viewer, the artist or anyone else creates or destroys its meaning in the search for common reality. Yet creative art continually escapes, evades definition and follows an independent road: it is open to interpretation and reinterpretation until its decimated image can be recreated by the techniques of a craft.

In the creative mood an adult or child sheds knowledge of shared reality and enters an imaginative world where conscious intentions are left in abeyance. Profound emotions or playful feelings may emerge while hand and eye are occupied in partnership. In this mood there can be no mistakes or omissions because there has been no preconceived plan. The child or adult watches the effect of the material being handled as if it emerges by itself. At a certain point he or she may add something deliberately, such as a title, to link it to the outer world of shared reality, but then the creative process stops (Figure 3.4).

Figure 3.4 Boats, Past and Present, Traditional Linear

~~Kitchen artists do not paint to sell their work and so they are content~~
to leave it as a medium of self-communication; yet the satisfaction of
discovering an image in paint or clay is enhanced when someone else
enjoys the image and the creative whole, the individual self, is shown
beyond the socially acceptable persona.

In this sense I consider that Kitchen Art presents the essence of art as
therapy. The simple coming together of individuals for the exercise of
creative initiative has an effect upon mental health. Most people find little
need to be creative when life is not unduly stressed; but life is not always
benign, and when things go wrong many people yearn for a means of
achieving their needs and wishes. If their frustration is sufficiently intense
Kitchen Art can alleviate the immediate stress.

Some people join a Kitchen Art group temporarily but find that it does
not satisfy their need; they may be disturbed by the lack of external control
by means of technique and may thus prefer an evening class in art or
craftwork; others may come to feel a need for individual art therapy.

When we look at Kitchen Art in practice it may seem to be an
amateurish and hazy concept. Little more is provided than the kitchen,
the owner's love of creativity and a cup of tea or coffee when the session
ends. How can it be claimed as a provision for mental health? If we ask
them, the participants are unlikely to have any reasonable explanation. I
refer to some psychoanalytic writings for an explanation.

Michael Balint describes the self-sufficiency experienced by the adult
or child who discovers this means of uncovering and expressing his deepest
needs and wishes as:

the area of creation ... in it there is no external object present. The subject is on his own and his main concern is to produce something out of himself.

(Balint 1986: 24)

The need for images creates dreams, formed when the conscious mind sleeps at night. Freud, who studied dreams so thoroughly describes them as the precursors of verbal thought:

our thoughts originated in such perceptual forms; their earliest material and the first stages in their development consisted in sense impressions or, more accurately, as memory pictures of these. It was later that words were attached to these pictures and then connected so as to form thoughts. In the course of this *regression* all new acquisitions won during this development of memory pictures into thoughts must necessarily fall away.

(Freud 1961: 152; emphasis in original)

Freud considers dreaming as a temporary regression, an undoing of logical sequences of daytime thought but Balint takes this idea further when he says:

On the whole, most things, objects, relationships, emotions and so on can be expressed equally well in the various languages. I would emphasize that most of them *can*, because some of them can *not*. This is particularly true of emotionally highly charged communications. Good examples of this kind are lyric poetry or words sung to music: to translate any of these is an almost impossible task. My favourite explanation of this difficulty uses the idea of a 'cluster of associations' that surrounds each word and is different in every language, different even in varying human relationships using the same language.

(Balint 1986: 92; emphasis in original)

The symbolic imagery of art carries this limitless cluster of associations; the artist is not tied to the logical structure of rational communication. Moreover, the point is made that intense emotions cannot be framed in words alone; to this I would add the whole area of inarticulate sensuous life that demands recognition even from birth.

Michael Balint marks the importance of creative art as a means of making intelligible what may be generally unintelligible:

as far as we know the unconscious has no vocabulary in our sense; although words exist in it, they are neither more or less than any object representation, they do not yet possess the overriding symbolic function that they will acquire in adult language. They are mainly pictures, images, sounds which may without much ado change their meaning or merge into each other as they do, in fact, in dreams.

(Balint 1986: 97)

Jeff, who had always been short of words, was unceasingly imaginative in his symbolic imagery of things – objects, relationships, emotions and the sensuous, aesthetic delights of colour and shape. He presented these unspoken thoughts with the assurance of a man who habitually thought in images rather than words. In everyday life this was a serious handicap, but it was a direct advantage in painting, making him the envy of some who found that ideas could get in the way of their creativity.

Without art and dreams we have to rely on crude signals, looks or gestures, acted out to those who must interpret them intuitively when the word cannot be taken for the deed; art is needed if we are to communicate that which cannot be said in mere words.

Kitchen Art affirms the right to play. Here Winnicott helps us to look deeply into the processes of play and its importance in psychotherapy:

> The searching [for the Self] can come only from desultory formless functioning, or perhaps from rudimentary playing, as if in a neutral zone. It is only here, in this unintegrated state of the personality, that that which we describe as creative can appear. This, if reflected back, *but only if reflected back*, becomes part of the organized personality, and eventually this in summation makes the individual to be, to be found; and eventually enables himself or herself to postulate the existence of the self. ... This gives us our indication for therapeutic procedure – to afford an opportunity for formless experience, and for creative impulses, motor and sensory, which are the stuff of playing. And on the basis of playing is built the whole of man's experiential existence. No longer are we either introvert or extravert. We experience life in the area of transitional phenomena, in the exciting interweave of subjectivity and objective observation, and in the area that is intermediate between the inner reality of the individual and the shared reality of the world that is external to individuals.
>
> (Winnicott 1971: 64; emphasis in original)

Kitchen Art does not aim to create art objects but to discover the 'formless experience' of creative impulses, motor and sensory, which are the stuff of playing. Play is a profound experience of inner reality that belongs together with the ability (at another time) to use assumptions about the external world of shared reality. For a couple of hours in someone's kitchen we are free from the pressures of social correspondences and can paint with the freedom of a child.

With the ever-increasing specialization of art therapy, Kitchen Art is an opportunity for the artist in the therapist to keep in touch with his or her own creativity. Without adequate exercise of our creative art capacity it is too easy to erect a false barrier of psychological interpretation that makes all art – including our own – pathologically suspect. There is a real danger that we project our own need to be creative upon the therapeutic situation so that we make it our own work of art.

THE KITCHEN AND THE COMMUNITY

The steady response to art as therapy over the years strengthened my conviction of the need for people not clinically ill to have opportunities for play with such undemanding materials as paint and clay, as distinct from the object-making requirements of art and craft constructions that demand traditional skills.

Throughout the following chapters I shall present the therapeutic need for creative initiative as the complement to the ability to co-operate with others in the various recreative ways necessary for viable society. The principle could be formulated crudely, as 'the more you have to take in, the more you need to put out'.

Living demands a great deal from the individual in teaching and learning, and an overemphasis on taking in and putting oneself out can lead to an illness that Winnicott defines as 'compliance':

> It is assumed here that the task of reality-acceptance is never completed, that no human being is free from the strain of relating inner and outer reality, and that relief from this strain is provided by an intermediate area of experience (Riviere, 1936) which is not challenged. This intermediate area is in direct continuity with the play area of the small child who is 'lost in play'.
>
> (Winnicott 1971: 13)

There is a need for creative expression rather than the abundance of classes and courses in recreation that are pervaded by the demands of external reality. Recreation is not the same as relaxation and here, again, I rely upon Winnicott to put the difference succinctly:

> I am trying to refer to the essentials that make relaxation possible. In terms of free association this means that the patient on the couch or the child patient among the toys on the floor must be allowed to communicate a session of ideas, thoughts, impulses and sensations that are not linked except in some way that is neurological or physiological and perhaps beyond detection.
>
> (Winnicott 1971: 55)

He goes on to say that relaxation creates nonsense and that there is a place for a trusted therapist or friend to take nonsense as indirect communication and:

> In these highly specialized conditions the individual can come together and exist as a unit, not as a defence against anxiety but as an expression

of I AM, I am alive, I am myself. From this position everything is creative.

(Winnicott 1971: 56)

In Kitchen Art we can share a common goal and resolve the troubling question 'When is a patient not a patient?' In the kitchen the therapist can also paint and use clay, relieving him or her of envy aroused when patients have the special conditions where they can freely paint, an opportunity for de-specialization, where patient and professional alike are free of the formal setting of a consulting room or studio. If the kitchen artist needs a modelling tool or a palette there are plates and cutlery to hand.

For me Kitchen Art groups provided an important link between my earliest experiences of art therapy and its development in social psychiatry, special education and the Health and Social Services.

KITCHEN ART'S PRECURSOR

I began to offer opportunities for spontaneous painting and drawing for untrained adults and children in my own premises in London at a time when war had created many exceptional hazards. My own ignorance of psychopathology seemed invaluable, all was new and untried and these small groups showed the particular value of an unstructured setting where this very ignorance (of mine) was relaxing and enjoyable for some troubled people recovering from or sustaining a mental illness. When I was given the use of premises the patients helped to furnish and equip two rooms. Some of their doctors were interested in the art work, others were not, and the openness of this situation had at least one unexpected result when an old tramp included himself in my group and painted regularly for many months, eventually retiring to the regular profession of pavement artist.

Within this setting I learnt something of the Adlerian principles of social therapy in creative art groups but, being an artist, I could not use the notion of art specifically as a group therapy, although I could see that undertaking an individual pursuit in company with other, like-minded individuals created an unspoken bond between us in our need to integrate the inner and outer realities of our lives.

Kitchen Art is not an art class or a form of individual/group psychotherapy, nor is it art therapy. Where is its place in the sustenance of mental health? The participants are not patients, although stress must be presumed to release creative art activity. Kitchen Art groups have included an artist, a social worker, an occupational therapist, a scientist, a surgeon and an art therapist, painting, writing poetry or shaping clay beside children, ex-psychiatric patients and people with physical and mental disabilities. All come without their professional or social skills and responsibilities, having no reports to write, no schemes to operate and no duties beyond the common need to share the milieu.

When I share Kitchen Art sessions I am able to return for a few hours to myself, my hands and eyes, responding thoughtlessly to shapes and colours, the whole of me that is usually de-integrated when learning, reading or responding to someone. In freely created work I renew my trust in myself to shape and integrate inner and outer needs.

PRACTICALITIES

Kitchen Art responds to a need that is not clinically identified, a need that falls within the non-specific condition of stress in everyday life. How, then is its undefined therapeutic aim maintained?

The balance between the needs of inner and outer reality defines the mental health of any individual or group. The weight inevitably falls on the individual's need to maintain shared reality, even if it blocks or limits the personal freedom to withdraw into the exclusive area of creativity. Kitchen Art can provide a setting for this imbalance to be rectified, where most of the time is given to the uniqueness of the inner world.

The principle of Kitchen Art overlaps with that of art therapy in providing the maximum freedom for self-expression within a cohesive group. A typical example is given in Chapter 5 on art as therapy in a Social Services' children's home, where vacant rooms on the premises were used as an art club for the children, some of whom had been in individual art therapy in a different setting.

The convenor of a group may be the owner of the kitchen, but the purpose of the group is maintained by members who protect it against internal and external social pressures. Such impulses to maintain attention to the inner world seem to come spontaneously from the group rather than to depend upon any qualification. If this does not occur, the creative impetus is lost and the members flounder, caught in a need for external qualification, buying books on art or technique and fading away into an amateur art class.

External pressures may come from the host setting, particularly if this has moved beyond the kitchen to an organization such as a church, a charity or some part of the local Health and Social Services rehabilitative programme, such as mobility classes for the sight impaired, heart and stroke clubs, Cruse or the NSPCC.

I have found that mixed groups of adults and children from the same neighbourhood work well together through the opportunity to play with paint or clay during a village festival. All these opportunities for free, creative activity are vulnerable to our social need to create and develop meaning in outer life. While it can be contained within the group, the inner life can be expressed and the balance maintained between the two realities.

I leave the last word on this to Winnicott:

Of every individual who has reached the stage of being a unit with a linking membrane and an outside and an inside it can be said that there is an *inner reality* to that individual, an inner reality that can be rich or poor and can be at peace or in a state of war. This helps, but is it enough?

My claim is that if there is a need for this double statement, there is also a need for a triple one: the third part of the life of a human being, a part that we cannot ignore is an intermediate area of *experiencing*, to which inner and external life both contribute. It is an area that is not challenged, because no claim is made on its behalf except that it shall exist as a resting place for the individual engaged in the perpetual human task of keeping inner and outer reality separate yet interrelated.

(Winnicott 1971: 2; emphasis in original)

Figure 3.5 A community art marathon

SUMMARY

Although Kitchen Art is not a form of group therapy where the troubled inner world is discussed, creative playfulness can be enhanced when several people work in the same room or even on a single piece of paper. Figure 3.5 shows an example of creative play in a local street festival. Kitchen Art is one way of establishing a situation where adults and children can be freely creative. This is a version of an old idea that mental health concerns both body *and* mind, head *and* heart, psyche *and* soma. Some examples have been given the use of Kitchen Art in alleviating stress before it becomes a clinical problem.

REFERENCES

Balint, M. (1986) *The Basic Fault*, London: Tavistock.

Bierer, J. (1944) *Therapeutic Social Clubs: Developments in Social Psychiatry as Formulated by Joshua Bierer*, London: Institute of Social Psychiatry.

Bierer, J. and Evans, R. (1969) *Innovations in Social Psychiatry*, London: Avenue Publishing Company.

Freud, S. (1961) *Introductory Lectures on Psycho-analysis*, London: Allen & Unwin.

Simon, R. M. (1944) *The Art Circle, in Therapeutic Social Clubs*, London: J. K. Lewis & Company.

Winnicott, D. W. (1971) *Playing and Reality*, London: Tavistock.

Chapter 4

Peter and other physically handicapped people

What I say does affect our view of the question: what is life about? You may cure your patient and not know what it is that makes him or her go on living. It is of first importance for us to acknowledge openly that the absence of psycho-neurotic illness may be health, but it is not life. Psychotic patients who are all the time hovering between living and not living force us to look at this problem, one that really belongs not to psycho-neurotics but to all human beings.

(Winnicott 1971: 100)

Every individual needs to balance inner and outer life in order to accommodate the circumstances of change. In this chapter I describe the way in which Peter and some other people used art as a means of balancing their inner lives against a drastic change from normal health to crippling disability.

PETER

Years ago I was asked to work with a seventeen-year-old boy who had suffered for ten years from a degenerative neuro-muscular condition that was first diagnosed when, as a young child, he began to fall down. By the time he was fourteen he was almost completely lacking voluntary movement, only able to move his right arm and hand to some extent and the muscles of his face and neck. He could not speak and found it difficult to swallow. He was emaciated and was not expected to live much longer, although he was able to stay at home with his parents in the country.

As it took me a whole working day to complete a visit, Peter was offered a two-hour session once a fortnight. His only means of communication was by smiling, refraining from smiling or by rolling his head back to imitate a laugh. A forbidding look indicated his disagreement. When I was stupid enough to ask two questions at once he would roll back his head and laugh at me soundlessly.

As we got to know each other I was greatly rewarded by Peter's smile and disappointed by its absence – these were the only means I had of understanding how he felt. As a young boy he had enjoyed painting small watercolour landscapes, and when I saw these I wondered how he would feel when he found that he could no longer use this skill. Clearly, we would both need to find a different way of working, for normally I did not intervene in patients' art nor did I talk very much during a session; now, I would have to ask in order to understand what Peter wanted, and I would have to do a great deal for him, which meant that I must follow his directions. To do this properly I had to discover the questions that I needed to ask so that he could answer with a smile.

Because Peter was so very limited in means of expression, if art was to be therapy I had to meet his creative needs as closely as possible. It was not my job to decide what he could or could not do. He was alert and full of mental energy, only lacking the physical strength to sketch or write. In similar ways, working with small children had shown me the benefits of 'role reversal' when they dictated stories before they could write.

As far as I could tell, Peter did not discover images by free painting; his temperament and circumstances, mind and body needed a plan that could be changed later. This meant that I had to do a lot of the work that his hand could not do, without taking the initiative from him. Much time had to be spent finding out what he wanted to do by shaping questions that could be answered simply by his 'yes' smile, or the opposite.

I discovered that Peter wanted to paint big pictures in oils, which meant that we had to invent a new way of working. First, I would divide a sheet of drawing paper into a variety of rectangles, each about 3 inches in diameter and Peter would choose the shape he preferred and draw a few lines in it with felt-tipped pen; then I had to find out what he intended the lines to be.

I could not tell if he planned these paintings or just used the lines to focus his reverie; whether he was making an abstract pattern or trying to achieve an image. Anyhow, I continued guessing aloud until he smiled; then I had to find out the size he envisaged and mechanically enlarge his lines on the rigid surface of a card or board.

Next there were decisions to be made about colours he needed me to mix; it helped a lot if Peter could tell me whether the face, landscape or still life was imagined to be in day or night, sun, cloud or rain. When I had got the colour he wanted I mixed several tones of it and he smeared these together to get an effect, pushing his brush across the palette in a way that was more skilful than it seemed. Luck was usually on his side, but when it failed he might overpaint or I would painstakingly remove the offence. As we had two hours for work, the discussions were enjoyable and neither of us became impatient about the time needed for preparation.

Each painting took about eight sessions, about sixteen hours to complete. Later, he had to come to terms with muscular spasms that could introduce unexpected extras. Peter was very upset by this at first and I could only tell him that it was not my job to alter anything until he, like any other artist, had discovered his limitations and had chosen which marks to keep, whether they had been made by accident or not.

He usually chose to paint on a shape that was about 12 or 15 inches square and this posed a problem, as he had not the strength to stretch his arm away from his body even with a long brush bound to his hand. However, he had no difficulty in pushing the brush up from the bottom of the board to the middle, then I could turn it round and he would paint the side or the top from the bottom up. We had no difficulty in envisaging the picture in this way, or in imagining it as the right way up while he was painting upwards from his lap.

I invited Peter to use a quick-drying oil in his paint so that he could have better control in smearing the colours together to get the tints and tones he needed from those I prepared on the palette to his instructions.

Later, as Peter's arm became weaker, I knelt beside him and supported his wrist with my hand; feeling the slight contraction of his tendons I could follow his minute efforts to direct the brush.

PETER'S ART STYLES

Peter's original art had been conceptual, in the Traditional Linear style, with each small landscape carefully thought out with bright colours and neat detail (Plate 10). These paintings, made two or three years before, were remarkably controlled, and I think his original tendency to plan now helped him to adjust to the rather tortuous method we had to invent. When he decided to use oils I was pleased, for this medium is more flexible than watercolour.

With the change of medium Peter made changes in style and subject-matter also; a painting of imaginary flowers was formalized with angular shapes, a huge face broken into dramatic planes. Then he painted a figure in slightly smaller scale set in a landscape against a dark mass that seemed to support it (Figure 4.1). Peter chose to entitle this painting *Jumping Out*. I saw this as a self-portrait that expressed, by its Archaic distortion, an inner energy that could only be expressed in his face.

The first two paintings were made in large flat areas of colour, a transition between the Linear and Massive styles; but *Jumping Out* had a smaller scale and the effect of flattened space (stage and backdrop) included some traditional pictorial values.

After these, Peter retained the smaller scale in landscape paintings, adding detail to the outlines I had enlarged from the few strokes he had made. He began to choose smaller panels for painting and, by the brilliance of his smiles, I understood his need for the subtle tones and shades of naturalism to express the changes in light that gave variety to the

Figure 4.1 Jumping Out, Massive transition

familiar landscape (Plate 11). He painted from memory a misty hollow, which was a remarkable recollection by any standard.

Peter's disability had left his mental state unimpaired. His mind was clear and his interest in life reached outward as far as his disease permitted and also inward to his need to use creative initiative in painting. His first Archaic paintings symbolized the importance of inner reality. His mother called these works 'Modern Art' and Peter seemed to enjoy the freedom of that idea. His later works, smaller in size and scale and more naturalistic, are in the area of Traditional naturalism; they are visual impressions of the landscapes he saw on family outings, set in specific seasons and weathers that we worked out through my questions.

I felt that it was particularly important for Peter to visualize as clearly as possible when he began to use the later style, although, of course, discussions about a scene, its weather, time of year, and so on, would have been distracting and intrusive at the earlier, Archaic phase, in which he was expressing emotional and sensuous values that are universal, without any specific time or place.

As Peter's condition deteriorated further, his Traditional art style became less Massive and included some of the Linear emphases that had been his adolescent art style. These elements of clarity and neatness gave his last landscapes a sort of idealism, a conceptual quality that I guessed to be the final resource against his tragic condition.

PETER'S ART AS THERAPY

My work with Peter taught me a new way of using art as therapy. Peter was mentally healthy and strong and needed painting to redress the balance between his mental and physical life. This he could do if I met his physical needs. To do this I had to supply words to indicate my understanding and eventually I even had to supplement the weakened muscles of his arm.

Peter was recommended for art therapy by the Social Services because his physical condition and isolation were very stressful but I could not see that he suffered from a mental illness. He seemed to me to have adjusted supremely well to the extremely narrow confines of his physical condition, and his first use of art showed positive emotion towards external life. Any spontaneous, direct handling of colour/tone in broad sweeping gestures, any impulsive, psycho-physical acts were impossible, and his feelings were first expressed through strong, hot colours and diagonal, geometric shapes in flower painting and simple landscapes that gave a sense of precarious equilibrium.

The early months spent on these first Archaic paintings seemed, miraculously, to release the frail energy I saw in the lively, gnome-like figure that leaps, yet rests against a background shape that reminds me of the big armchair Peter sat in to paint (Figure 4.1).

When, later, he turned his mind's eye to perceptual recollections, his style became naturalistic and showed exceptional subtlety. During the years when physical deterioration was minimal he made a number of small paintings that he wanted to be exhibited and sold without the buyer knowing of the way they were made. Then, as he became weaker, the sense of space and atmosphere was lost. I could not tell how far this was caused by my insensitivity to his increasing dependence on my interventions; whatever the cause, the Linear emphasis became stronger, the detail sharper and he was less able to improvise and change. He easily tired and painting became a crude denial of his increasing helplessness.

To talk of transference and counter-transference in this situation seems like 'pathologizing' the natural affection that arose between us during four years of fortnightly visits; Peter remained an object of my concern for a while after weakness and sedation had finally destroyed his hold on life. He died having lived most of his last four years beyond medical expectation.

Apart from the physical interventions I have described, I also stepped beyond the therapeutic role when I arranged a public exhibition for twenty-three landscapes – eight were sold.

Although Peter's creative need was to make pictures, art alone would not have been enough. He needed to be in charge of his art, even though dependent on practical help; he needed to know that I would do nothing without his explicit instructions, however long it might take me to understand them.

Peter taught me a great respect for his defences; his unremitting enthusiasm for his paintings demanded that each one had to be completed and framed according to his choice. Before meeting Peter I had worked with adults and children who were concerned with their inner world in paint or clay, but Peter was eager to give a public face to his art. Kramer (1973) gives thorough attention to the importance of fully formed creative expression for disturbed children and Winnicott (1971: 43–6) considers repetitive play to have similar, ego-enhancing value.

In order to make his paintings, Peter had to take a positive attitude towards his body and its infirmities before he could adapt my interventions as his tools. Once he could accept help in mixing colour and enlarging scribbles, he was able to change them freely and to tolerate involuntary alterations caused by the spasms without distress. Unlike the paintings he made at school, he came to let pictures develop in unexpected ways, beyond the limitations of our laborious preparations, and thus he could create art through the body use that remained available to him.

As I understand it, the task of working with physically ill and disabled adults and children makes special demands upon the art therapist's creativity as an artist. The art therapist must respond to the non-verbal signals that indicate the other person's creative needs. Although intuition is an essential part of any therapeutic intervention, it has a particularly delicate role to play in situations where help for a disabled person can so easily become intrusive. Creative initiative can become a double-edged sword. Winnicott spoke of this danger of doing too much for the patient through interpretation, but there can be a similar danger in helping the patient to paint:

> If only we can wait, the patient arrives at understanding creatively and with immense joy, and I now enjoy this joy more than I used to enjoy the sense of having been clever.
>
> (Winnicott 1971: 86)

Peter's painting gave him intense joy; even when I mistook his intentions and mixed the wrong colour, he was happy enough to laugh at me and wait until I had got it right.

ART THERAPY WITH SOME
OTHER PHYSICALLY DISABLED PATIENTS

The value of creative art in the treatment of physical illness was first recognized by Florence Nightingale:

> The effect in sickness of beautiful objects, of variety of objects and especially brilliancy of colour is hardly at all appreciated. ... People say the effect is only on the mind. It is no such thing. The effect is on the body too. Little as we know about the way in which we are affected by form, by colour and light, we do know this, that they have an actual physical effect.

(Nightingale 1860)

Artists were first invited to work with patients in hospital when wartime conditions threatened to break down the existing medical and psychiatric provision. Due to the unremitting efforts of Adrian Hill, the recognition of creative art for long-stay physically ill patients was recognized as a psychological therapy, rather than an occupation or mere recreation.

Adrian Hill was an art teacher whose recovery from pulmonary tuberculosis after surgery had been exceptionally successful. His doctors considered this to be due to his ability to absorb himself in creative art, and they asked him to help other patients in sanatoria to paint (Hill 1941) and to recruit artists to work in this way. In 1944 Adrian, through the National Association for the Prevention of Tuberculosis, invited me to provide art therapy sessions in a number of TB units in general hospitals, and this led to its use in surgical and neurological wards, and in one sanatorium.

Adrian had experienced the psychological effects of the disease and the enforced idleness its treatment entails and, although I did not have this special knowledge, I had been a sickly child, often confined to bed, and was therefore interested in the idea of extending my experience of art therapy with psychiatric patients to work with others who also had to cope with isolation, weakness and fever. Three examples of paintings by patients suffering pulmonary tuberculosis show how their styles express their prevailing attitudes:

Figure 4.2.   *Playing Ball* is an Archaic Massive watercolour symbolizing a typically hyperactive response to enforced bedrest.

Figure 4.3   *A Black Vista* is a Traditional Linear poster painting of remembered landscape by a young man who was dangerously ill.

Figure 4.4   *Time Out* is a Traditional Massive oil painting by a medical student frustrated rather than frightened by her disease.

Figure 4.2 Playing Ball, Archaic Massive (TB patient)

Figure 4.3 A Black Vista, Traditional Linear (TB patient)

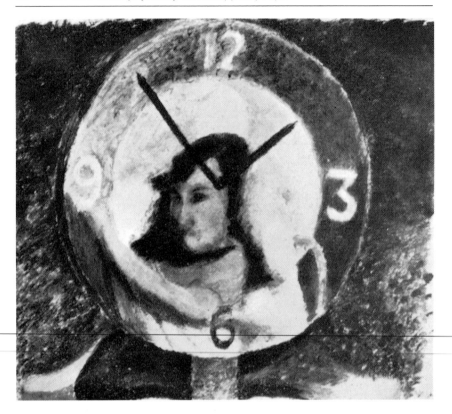

Figure 4.4 Time Out, Traditional Massive (TB patient). From A. Hill, *Painting Out Illness* (1951), Williams & Norgate

As I began to work for the newly formed Health and Social Services, further areas of need were discovered. Blind people can paint and model clay if we take the trouble to find out enough of their physical and psychological needs. One blind woman had the idea of drawing her pictures with ropes of clay; she could feel these with her brush and fill the spaces with colours that had been described to her in detail. If dark paper is used, the spaces where the ropes had lain can look like the leading between painted glass. A sight-impaired woman used her residual sight to make a delicate seascape of a storm-tossed boat and another incised a flower picture in a slab of clay and painted the plaster cast as wall plaque.

Figure 4.5 is a good example of the confidence that creative initiative can restore, in this case through visual recollection of a scene that was important to an old man who had been without sight for twenty years.

He wanted to make a picture of his cottage garden and thought that this would best be done by modelling clay. However, when he found difficulty in making the flowers and shrubs he asked for the base panel of clay to be flattened so that he could draw on it. Then he took the round lid of his tobacco tin and pressed this into the clay to shape the little pond he

Figure 4.5 My Cottage Garden, Traditional Linear

had made long ago, and then drew his thatched cottage at the top of the panel and added a row of gladioli in front. When I had cast this for him he was able to tell me the colours he wanted to use to paint it. Finally, when it seemed finished, he exclaimed in great disappointment, 'I have forgotten to put in the poplar tree!' Taking a brush, he asked for green paint and added the tree neatly to the side of the cottage.

Anecdotes such as this are not useful as technical hints that can be applied to any patient who does not know what to do. If I am to adhere to the principle of art as therapy I must only offer simple materials; any tricks or techniques must arise from creative initiative if they are to have a therapeutic effect. As Winnicott notes:

> [Analysts] need to beware lest they create a feeling of confidence and an intermediate area in which play can take place, and then inject into this area or inflate it with interpretations which, in effect, are from their own creative imaginations.
>
> (Winnicott 1971: 102)

I think this warning applies to the therapist who unintentionally drifts into the position of teacher. The lines between art therapy, art teaching and psychotherapy can be extremely faint and it is not always easy to observe the boundaries. Failure to recognize boundaries is an intrusion upon the patient's creativity – even if he or she is polite enough to invite us it is still a betrayal of trust. Trust is essential, not only the patient's trust in him or herself, but also the therapist's trust in the innate human creativeness that we all can enjoy.

I had to learn to be actively helpful to patients who were physically handicapped, ill or disabled without allowing my own creativity to lead the way. It is really a question of allowing oneself to be used as a tool, since art as therapy collapses if control of the art work is taken away, even for a moment; for the patient loses touch with the continuity of his preconscious imagery and is forced to see the work through my eyes, as an object in external reality. This forces a premature birth of the symbolic image, as it is forced to declare itself as a sign of something. The patient loses unthinking trust in him- or herself and can take a long time to recover the uncontaminated mental space needed for creative work. The instance I have given, of the blind man who added his poplar tree weeks after he had completed his picture, illustrates an exceptional achievement in recovering the intensity of a recollection.

Winnicott writes of the imaginative life as the area of illusion in which any impingement is a trespass:

> The potential space between baby and mother, between child and family, between individual and the world depends on experience which leads to trust. It can be looked upon as sacred to the individual in that

it is here that the individual experiences creative living. By contrast, exploitation of this area leads to a pathological condition in which the individual is cluttered up with persecutory elements of which he has no means of ridding himself. It may perhaps be seen from this how important it can be for the analyst to recognize the existence of this place where play can start.

(Winnicott 1971: 103)

Freely creative activity in drawing, painting, claywork or writing is possible despite interventions by the therapist if these interventions are practical necessities elicited and directed by the patient. The difference between therapy and technical instruction depends upon the therapist's ability to follow the patient's lead.

Our psychosomatic integrations are particularly clear in spontaneous responses to drawing and painting, where physical postures and movements are needed to discover the image. These are expressed by the artist's body, its particular qualities as 'handwriting' and its limitations. Equally, the patient's freedom of mind is reflected in the use of arm, hand and eye, the way of sitting or standing or shifting about. Figures 4.2, 4.3 and 4.4 are examples of this spontaneous 'body language', transmitted to the art material, that expresses the patient's attitude towards life at the time the paintings were made. Working with some patients suffering from Parkinson's disease, I found that their focused attention to painting reduced their tremors and, similarly, some stroke patients were able to perform movements that had not been restored by physiotherapy (Simon 1988).

The results of creative initiative flow over into other areas of the patient's attitude to life (Simon 1991: 129–30), but convalescence can bring its own difficulties. The return to family and social life may decentralize the stress of illness, yet convalescence has anxieties that contribute to the form of the art, clearly indicated in the art of the patient John, who responded to his recovery by a temporary regression to the unconventionality of his earlier, Archaic transitional style of art (Simon 1991), indicating a need for as slow a weaning from art therapy as for any other situation involving dependence.

Some patients respond to their return to everyday life by accentuating the Traditional features of their art work, sometimes causing a secret disappointment for the artist in the therapist. Adrian Hill noted this in the earliest written record of art as therapy:

In more than one case I have noticed a curious psychological metamorphosis in subject matter during the return of a patient's health to normal. When their physical resistance is at its lowest, their powers of imagination often rise to a very high level: the patient demonstrating his recovery by a gradual descent to a pictorial commonplace.

(Hill 1941: 41)

As well as a means of meeting deep psychological suffering, art is a therapy for adults and children who have always lived with severe handicaps and have developed positive defences against their condition. Peter (mentioned earlier) and other patients such as Barbara (Chapter 7) taught me the value of these defences and the use of creativity in extending them.

An art teacher for physically handicapped children gave me a precise example of this use of freely created art in a specialized setting. Maureen Cashell, an art teacher and associate of Art Therapy in Northern Ireland pioneered the use of art therapy alongside National Curriculum teaching. She was able to set up a voluntary art club, which ran weekly after normal school hours, using the spacious amenities of the Domestic Science department. In a setting that was not, in some ways, as appropriate as the regular art room, Maureen noticed that wheelchairs and all other mechanical aids that the children needed for normal schoolwork were left outside the door when they came to paint: then they used the bodies they had, as they actually were, in order to meet their need for creative expression; Maureen was needed only to provide art materials and to protect their physical safety. Her enthusiasm for this project and the concerned attention she gave to the children's freedom of expression had considerable value in fostering the children's sense of self-worth and individuality.

The release of creative initiative in art work has a positive value in rehabilitation, not only through improving the quality of life in a general sense but in some physical ways as well. For instance, some stroke patients who were at first unable to complete one side of a painting would, over a period of months, spontaneously 'edge' their pictures further into the vacant space. During a ten-day introduction to art as therapy for a group of people with Parkinson's disease I found that the severe tremors that several group members suffered abated when they were actually drawing or painting. One patient in particular, although severely disabled and unable to speak clearly or stand unaided, could paint with large, sweeping strokes and could also make small, detailed drawings.

SUMMARY

Art therapy for physically ill and disabled patients has a beneficent effect upon the mind and the body: it is visible evidence of the uniqueness of individual experience.

Since these far-off days, many more ways treating the stress of long, dangerous or terminal illness or disability have been developed, here and in other countries, but it still seems important to emphasize the essential difference between art and other forms of therapy.

Of all the great variety of human needs the most desperate is the need, from birth onwards to define the Self and to relate to others, especially in times when the Self, whether adult, child or baby, feels in danger of losing its identity in the face of external circumstances. The essence of creativity lies in the joy of awareness creative activity can bring, for none can paint another's picture or shape another's sculpture or write another's poem.

REFERENCES

Hill, A. (1945) *Art versus Illness*, London: Allen & Unwin.
—— (1951) *Painting out Illness*, London: Williams & Norgate.
Kramer, E. (1973) *Art as Therapy with Children*, London: Elek.
Nightingale, F. (1860) *Nursing: What it is and What it is not.*
Simon, R. M. (1988) Unpublished report for the Parkinson's Disease Society.
—— (1991) *The Symbolism of Style*, London: Routledge.
Winnicott, D. W. (1971) *Playing and Reality*, London: Tavistock.
—— (1971) *Therapeutic Consultations in Child Psychiatry*, London: Hogarth.

Chapter 5

Art therapy with children in residential care

To get the idea of playing it is helpful to think of the preoccupation that characterized the playing of a young child. The content does not matter. What matters is the near-withdrawal state, akin to the *concentration* of older children and adults. The playing child inhabits an area that cannot be easily be left, nor can it easily admit intrusions.

(Winnicott 1971: 51; emphasis in original)

It is important to my approach to art therapy with children or adults that I keep in mind the quality of free play between one art form and another. Painting and drawing are actions, and action can be mime, can lead on to words, stories and poems. Stories can be told with pictures or images that act out, or sing; the figures may be painted, given possessions, a setting, or dressed up: one child's fantasy may ring a bell and lead a group.

Children who have to be taken into long-stay care suffer in many ways. Not only have they the pain of separation from family and all the familiar things that went to make their everyday lives, but they face society's judgement upon their carers as having been unfit to look after them.

Long-term residential care aims to provide a physically healthy and safe environment modelled on the idea of normal life. However, it is not really a normal life, and some children are already too disturbed by their previous experiences to make positive use of it.

Although there are therapeutic residences, such as the Mulberry Bush, designed to face this problem in child care, my own approach to art therapy with some of these children has been within the more usual framework. Some children appear to adapt very well while others withdraw into false compliance or break out unexpectedly in panic, rage, nightmares or other symptoms of deep distress. A child can rarely explain why he or she runs away, steals, smokes, does badly at school or lashes out, and it is very frightening to be in the grip of an alien mood – to be 'beside oneself'. The child wants bad behaviour to be forgotten as soon as possible and the carers, if they cannot get to the bottom of it, also want to forgive and forget.

I first began to work with individual children in my office at a health centre. Children came there, or were brought to the studio at my home, by their care worker. Each child I saw was causing considerable concern by absconding, or school-refusing, glue-sniffing, smoking, committing vandalism or unprovoked violence. Others suffered persistent nightmares, were accident-prone or withdrawn. Each of these children showed physical signs of stress, being extremely tense and thin, or pale and flaccid.

They were aged from six to fifteen. When they had been coming regularly for a few months of weekly individual sessions, the staff found that they were easier to live with, less violent or withdrawn. It was considered beneficial for each of the children to have an hour a week for themselves, when they could use the art materials and talk to me as they wished. For this to be effective I had to be able to follow the symbolic meaning of the children's often non-verbal communications; when I could not, they were often deeply disappointed and temporarily reverted to their original behaviour. Sometimes I needed to join in their play, and indicate by this means that I was following what was going on. Talking directly about problems past or present was rarely necessary if the children assumed that I understood them and that I was as concerned as they were with what they were doing.

Without the clumsiness of words, my concerned attention acknowledged the importance of each child's self-image – a self-image that might be expressed as an animal, a house or a tree.

When I was asked to work with several children individually from the same residential home there was a special difficulty, for when a child improved, his or her place was given to another. Whereas children in ordinary family life have various means of working out their jealous feelings, such feelings could be intolerable for children who had already suffered a loss of intimate relationships. In response to this problem an art club was created on neutral premises where a child could continue to work with the art therapist alongside other children and adults. The club was to accommodate eight or nine children and I envisaged that this could give an opportunity for 'weaning' through their shared creative activities.

I had hoped that some of the residential staff would enjoy an opportunity to use the materials alongside the children, but after a few weeks it became clear that this arrangement was not practical. Staff cuts and duty hours made it impossible for anyone to attend regularly and this disappointed the children, who saw such absences as rejections. Moreover, some of the staff found difficulty in adopting a non-directive relation to the children. Free, unstructured art activity led some children to be more assertive than usual, and this meant that special techniques were needed for restoring their attention to their art.

As the group of eight or nine children was too big for me to manage on my own, I was extremely fortunate to find two volunteers who had art therapy experience. We each found slightly different roles and this arrangement spread the load very well. One of us naturally developed her approach on the lines of play therapy while the other, who ran an art therapy group in a geriatric hospital, enjoyed being with children who wanted to paint or use clay. We were given the use of two adjacent rooms in an unused part of the premises and, although the children were not limited to one or the other, there was a tendency for a child to stay with the same therapist's group for some time. With this splendid arrangement I was free to attend to the needs of any individual child who was in difficulties or who was disruptive.

The children found the sessions very satisfying. They usually worked separately, scattered about the rooms. Occasionally one or two children would share a common theme or even work together on one theme. For example, when one child made an elaborate clay pie, with clay plums

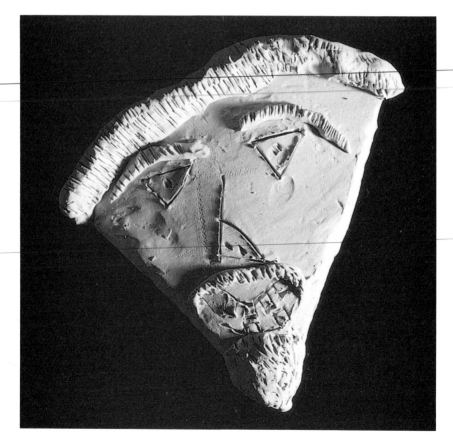

Figure 5.1 Face

inside the crust, the idea of food attracted others, who made clay plates and dishes of clay food, using the model as a two-dimensional image in the Archaic Linear style. These models were then painted. Some children preferred to flatten the clay and draw on it with a pencil, cutting out the picture as a flat panel, for example, a face (Figure 5.1). On another occasion two children pressed out flat discs as a pile of 'plates'; one plate became a desert island with a castaway and the bare necessities for survival (Figure 5.2), while Betty worked delicately, using the tips of her fingers

Figure 5.2 Desert Island

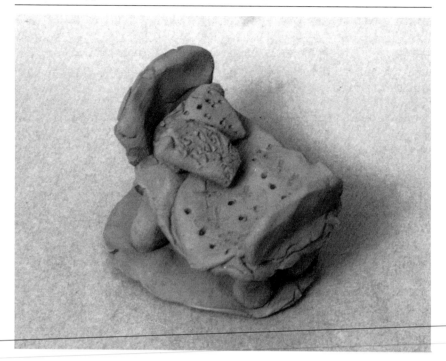

Figure 5.3 Bed with People

and sometimes a pencil, to model a tiny bedroom, with bed, dressing table and minute bedroom slippers (Figure 5.3).

Although the therapists talked to the children about their work, I did not feel that it would help them if anything we said unmasked their images by a direct reference to symbolic meaning. One reason for this is that I am always aware that a symbolic image, however obvious its meaning might appear to be, actually carries a multiplicity of meanings, most of which are beyond our conscious grasp at any particular time. Moreover, when we are able to sense some of these submerged ideas, it is often beyond our power to communicate them properly in words. If a child or anyone else describes a work of art the idea of it becomes fixed and the symbolic potential is lost.

NAMING, TELLING, INTERVENING

It is the privilege of the artist to name his or her work and thereby limit its associations to that name. Some children name directly when, for instance, a scribble is called 'That's my rage', but another child might use a similar scribble as a metaphor and can only tell me that 'a storm has broken up the house'. Other children seem to use the language of the primary process to bring a meaning towards the level of consciousness. For example, one child invented words for his pictures. I remember one scribble called 'Bilance Nice Poom' which might have been an anal euphemism using condensation and displacement.

In saying 'That's my rage', the first child acted out and recognized his action in the symbolic form of a painting; the child who sees a picture in her scribble has delayed *impulsive* expression of emotion: she is not acting *out* but acting within the therapeutic frame. If a child invents a name or tells a story for the symbolic image, he or she has further limited the sensuous or emotional impulse to an idea, removing it further still from direct action. These stages of transformation, from action to realization, provide different means of communication – the visual and the verbal. Both these means have a part to play in art therapy, but verbal communication limits the symbol to a definite meaning. Segal's distinction between symbolic equivalence and the symbol proper is a most useful description of the two activities being parts of the therapeutic process.

> I came gradually to the conclusion that one could differentiate between two kinds of symbol formation and symbolic function. In one, which I have called *symbolic equation* ... In the second case, that of true symbolism or *symbolic representation*, the symbol represents the object but is not entirely equated with it.
>
> (Segal 1991: 35; emphases in original)

The child who sees a story in her scribble invites the audience to add some details, but if they alter the painting this could be experienced as a tremendous intrusion, ending in a vicious fight; if the additions are words, these are a less obvious intrusion and can more easily be ignored; however, they will also tend to limit the symbol to thought. A child who has invented words, might feel lost in the scribble, as in a tangle of thought. Such an imitation of language is a great way to hide meaning and should be respected, but to its creator it can suddenly seem mad, a frightening experience of being 'beside oneself' and outside shared reality. The therapist is needed to help find a name, a boundary, a Circle to contain the riches of the image's manifold associations.

Intervention in play by an adult should be subservient, minimal. One successful intervention is described in my earlier book when the container was offered wordlessly, as a sponge (Simon 1991: 83). Rarely, a hidden association might seem crucial, and a therapist can help by drawing attention to it in some way. However, there is a danger in a loaded intervention because acting on a specific element may jump the gun, diverting our attention from the whole and the importance of waiting for the best time and form of interpretation:

> It is not the moment of my clever interpretation that is significant.
> Interpretation outside the ripeness of the material is indoctrination.
>
> (Winnicott 1971: 51)

This is not to say that hidden meanings must be ignored but that any response by a therapist is effective in the degree to which it fits the artist's own language and style. In *The Symbolism of Style* I gave detailed examples of interactive play with a young child. This play accepted the child's symbolic images as primary mental processes that were working slowly through the visual images towards secondary elaboration.

ART THERAPY AND ACTING

When art is a therapy it creates a tangible object that can be shared in contemplation. The way in which the work comes about informs the therapist. Unless patients use their acting *in* therapy and become aware of their actions as communications, they can only act *out*. This acting out shows the therapist something of how a patient may try to use the situation in order to continue behaving inappropriately. This is not itself therapeutic although it may prepare the way for therapy. After all, if the acting out has been the patient's usual way of dealing with life, one cannot expect an immediate change of heart.

For instance, one adolescent boy spent a long time painting a flag. He then repeatedly sprayed the painting with pastel fixative until the can was empty and he threw it away. It would have been offensive if I had *verbalized* the symbolism of the fixative while the flag was seen as a picture; it would, I think, have split the visual image of the Square (flag) he was trying to secure and taken away from him his opportunity for *visual* self-appraisal.

There are other ways of acting that come into art therapy. To act at all is to assert identity, while 'acting up' implies the assumption of a different or false identity. As dramatic art, acting is an enactment, calling on awareness of the Self as actor and the Other as audience.

Acting is an art form that allows children to express their feelings through the activity of their bodies. I find that unrehearsed acting has limited use in art therapy because it reaches so far beyond intention that it is often too close to acting *out* to have much therapeutic value. However, on at least one occasion it was possible to convert some acting into creative art by supplying an appreciative audience.

I remember one evening, at a time when the children's art club was deeply disturbed by external events. They were on the edge of anarchy – the children could not paint or use the clay except as a missile – and the group was only precariously held together by mutual affection, the children's secret need to avert their panic and rage, and the therapists' ability to keep our tempers. We were saved by Charlie, whose disruptiveness remained balanced between playfulness and violence. I encouraged him to repeat his act and hastily arranged chairs for the others as an audience. 'Acting out' suddenly became acting a series of short sketches in which the actors had to organize themselves to take turns.

UPTHRUST LEADERSHIP

Creative initiative appears in the art of children who work individually with me, and I can rely on it; but I was not so clear about the therapeutic possibilities for a group of damaged children. I was certainly unprepared for times when an otherwise inadequate child appeared to give voice and positive direction to the group's unconscious need for cohesion. I came to value this phenomenon and to distinguish it from a deliberate assumption of leadership.

We know that children in care need strong supportive help to deal with their tragic circumstances. If they cannot get the help they need they respond by reverting to their original stress signals – acting out violently or collapsing into withdrawal. When trouble and anxiety occurred within the residential home, the children came to the art club as usual but their creative initiative was seriously affected. Whole sessions became disturbed by moods of mistrust in our ability to understand. Few were able to resist this unsettled and destructive climate, nevertheless they all continued to attend, presumably hoping to recover their positive feelings. It was difficult to maintain a non-directive approach when so many children seemed to need us to represent the authority they deeply mistrusted.

On one occasion a near-riot ended when all the children ran off into the night. This was a matter of concern, for some of the children were known absconders. Within minutes they ran back again, carrying garden flowers they had ripped up. Someone stuck a flower stem into a lump of clay and within minutes they all took to the idea of making floral displays, some even shaping vases. I assume that the common aim originated from the initiative of one, unidentified child.

I came to see that an individual unconsciously reflects the immediate needs of the group: a destructive milieu producing an involuntary leader of its destructive needs and a positive, well-established group thrusting up a leader who briefly carries his or her group's positive expectation. I call this 'upthrust leadership' and see this as quite different from the role of a deliberately chosen, or self-appointed leader.

There was an impressive instance of 'upthrust' when Arthur, an accident-prone child, with his arm in plaster got on a table and announced that he was a pirate. This idea was taken up by the whole group, who immediately commandeered the table as a boat. The voyage attracted all eight children: the boys were pirates; the girls, slaves at the oars.

I thought that I could probably extend the effectiveness of this spontaneous play by offering to be a BBC commentator and could bring a tape-recorder the following week if they would do it again. I said, moreover, that as the performance could only be heard and not seen, they would have to make some background noises, such as waves or a gale.

At the next session they came prepared, wearing clothes they had cut and torn and with scars and cuts painted on their faces. I took the role of Radio Commentator, and Arthur, his arm still in plaster, manned the crow's nest. When he was finally persuaded to sight land, all the pirates disembarked and suddenly the fantasy collapsed; they could not imagine what could follow their arrival.

I felt I must intervene somehow and so I interviewed the Captain and asked what was to happen to the slaves – were they to be released? The pirates consulted each other and decided to marry them. There was a very brief group wedding which was seen as a satisfactory conclusion to the play and the children settled down to listen to the playback.

It was interesting to note that the pirates on this voyage met no hazards: no merchant ship or naval frigate attacked while they were steered by the lookout and rowed to safety by the slave girls; I wondered if this maiden voyage could lead on towards a less idealized vision of the future, sometime.

The phenomenon of brief, upthrust leadership seems an amoeba-like form of group behaviour – any part can be momentarily converted into a mouthpiece for the whole. On this occasion Arthur was the catalyst, although he was not at all a natural leader; rather, he was usually at the bottom of the pile, often seeming to be the focus of anyone's destructive feelings. When he set himself up by climbing on the table I found myself preparing to break his fall, but he became the focus of the group's initiative and, as lookout, piloted them to harbour. This self-regulating element in the children was totally unexpected but extremely valuable.

Our experience of part-time art therapy with groups of children in residential care brought forward several general issues that deepened our understanding of the effectiveness of therapeutic art groups for adults as well as children living in institutions. Given the unnatural situation of living away from home, creative art initiative has an immediate, positive value in situations where freedom of choice is often limited to the freedom to say 'no'. Although we encouraged the children to make whatever they liked with the paint and clay, we came to see that it was not the lack of restraint that helped them, but rather our implicit assumption that something positive would come from their activities. The upthrust leader may be the one who is most vulnerable to this assumption.

THE SYMBOLISM OF ACTING

I understand acting out as an involuntary use of others to hold on to oneself. In terms of the basic symbolism, such a Circle is only made by its lines of force, projected into the Square. I found that the style of the acts helped me to follow – and tolerate – potentially destructive group acting out. Such precariousness occurred at the time of the pirate's mass invasion of a single table/boat. Children were struggling to board or climb the rigging, others were rowing violently while the rest were drunken or rowdy pirates. Once again I refer to Winnicott, who has the words I need:

> Bodily excitement in erotogenic zones constantly threatens playing, and therefore threatens the child's sense of existing as a person. The instincts are the main threat to play as to the ego; in seduction some external energy exploits the child's instincts and helps to annihilate the child's sense of existing as an autonomous unit, making playing impossible.
>
> (Winnicott 1971: 52)

Therapeutic transformations from acting *out* into acting *in* can happen so quickly that they are easy to overlook, or misunderstand, especially in an anxious, hyperactive group. I think we often missed gems of positive initiative but often the therapeutic worth of some incident was personified in the upthrust leader rather than a child who was trying to conquer the group. For instance, Betty, who made the clay model of a young girl's bedroom, came to the art class for the first time on roller-skates (see p. 67).

Betty helped me to appreciate the quality of symbolic enactment as replay when she first arrived at the art club on roller-skates, successfully distracting everyone by the noise and violence of her entrance into the crowded room. She spoke in a deep voice and seemed to assume that she must break into the art club and assert herself manfully. When she had taken off her roller-skates the first work she made was in clay, roughly shaped as an elephant precariously balancing on an extremely small ball. The elephant was made from a hand-sized mass of clay that could easily have become a missile, and Betty's careless assurance in shaping it put the style into the Archaic Massive category, the style that expresses preoccupation with down-to-earth goodness and badness.

In due course Betty gravitated to the room where the occupational therapist had dolls and toys; there she used the sensitive help she found to develop a theme of doctors and nurses to work at her need to dominate and protect the ill toys. The change in her self-image was later confirmed by the Traditional style of her clay model of a young girl's bedroom (Figure 5.3).

SYMBOLS OF CIRCLES AND SQUARES

I have already indicated the importance that was given to the Circle as a symbol of Self when the children found some paper plates and distributed them to hold clay food. Betty preferred to use hers as the floor of a modelled bedroom (Figure 5.3) and another, Jennie, whom I write about in Chapter 8 on bereavement in children, set up an empty throne in the centre of her plate (Figure 5.4).

Considered in terms of basic symbolic images, Arthur's claim to one table as his territory seemed tantamount to claiming a Square. The mental space it implied was immediately invaded. This could have recreated a vicious circle of victim and persecutors, but I can only think that the time and place for this destructiveness was not right, for the children seemed to use the table as a Square, *en masse*. When they gathered around Arthur

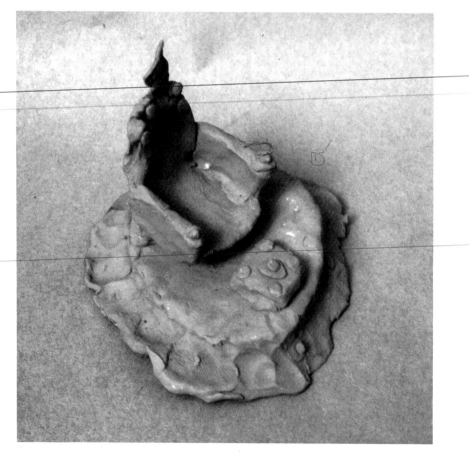

Figure 5.4 Throne

and did not attack him I imagined that this, one, extremely overcrowded table must have symbolized the imaginative space each child needed at that time. It was immediately important for me to recognize the meaning of the symbolism and, if necessary, to work to maintain it. When their act got going I had time to see that the boat could make a voyage; its symbolism could then incorporate ideas of space and time, intuitive/perceptive values of the Traditional Massive style and thus, within minutes, a chaotic manifestation of mass action (as an Archaic transition) had assumed a symbolic image of relatedness and group cohesion.

ART CLUB OR GROUP THERAPY?

Although I am not experienced in group therapy (for several individuals who happen to be working in the same room are not necessarily a group), it seemed to me that play-acting is what group therapy can be. My self-appointed task was to support its fragile containment by pretending to be a BBC commentator describing the scene.

SOME OF OUR QUESTIONS

As therapists we asked ourselves many questions. Should the art therapy that was happening be distinguished from group therapy and play therapy? Would it be useful to distinguish positive group interactions from the self-understanding that comes with an individual's deep absorption in creative art? The satisfaction of creating an image and seeing it appreciated by others often led to friendliness between the children, whether the subject of the work was pleasant or unpleasant. Could we compare the benefits of play-acting, with pre-existing 'props', with spontaneous creative art that only used pencils, paint or formless clay?

Could we convince anyone who had not been there that the art created was symbolic and that we were not imposing sophisticated adult ideas upon the children's mindless acts and objects?

How, for example, could a child's rough clay nest, full of crudely shaped nestlings, painted over and over again in grey-green and white, be *explained*? Does such an untutored art work help a child to deal with the practical issues of his life or only give a momentary escape from distress? Is the subject-matter an image of loss or the child's unrecognized potential?

Can we ever really know? I have not been a child in care, with that child's experience stretching back from the immediate moment into his past. As any one of these children stands holding a brush or a piece of clay I can only know how they seem to me and can only know their art as 'a subjective object'! It would be presumptuous to imagine that, through my knowledge and experience, I can really know the child as I can know a chair or a table. A workable understanding of any individual is almost entirely immediate and intuitive, however we manage to conceptualize our experience later.

POSSIBILITIES FOR RESEARCH

After two years of weekly sessions the art therapists were confident that we could present this unstructured way of working as a viable form of therapy and a research project, while running the art club in the same undirected way.

The Mental Health Foundation was approached and indicated an interest; however, by the time we had drawn up the formal application for a grant, things had changed. All children's residential homes had came under review and the effect of the inquiry was devastating for staff and children alike. The staff were suddenly full of anxiety and doubt, fearful of acting independently and the children were almost unmanageable. Within a few weeks the art club was closed down.

SUMMARY

An example is given of work in an art club for children in local authority care, designed on non-directive lines to help them use their experiences of individual art therapy to include sharing an open group in the same residential home.

Children in care are damaged by their experiences of family life but also by the inevitable deprivation resulting from social interventions. Consequently, they learn to mistrust authority and often try to force it to replicate their defences. Art as therapy can provide a means of escaping such vicious circles by discovering images in paint, clay, poetry and acting. The latter has immediate links with group therapy, but its effectiveness is weak if it leaves no permanent record. The children's positive use of the facility could only hold against the stable background of regular sessions which, over a period of two years, supported the children's fragile trust in their creativity.

REFERENCES

Segal, H. (1991) *Phantasy and Art*, London: Tavistock.
Simon, R. M. (1991) *The Symbolism of Style*, London: Routledge.
Winnicott, D. W. (1971) *Playing and Reality*, London: Tavistock.

Chapter 6

Images of depression in art therapy

Freely created art is autobiographical and, like a journal, reflects the mood of the creator. On one day we see our life in a way that may not be apparent on the next; our moods change, time and again.

This variability is more apparent in others than in ourselves; so strong is our present mood that we forget that we saw things otherwise or, if we recall another mood, we readily assume that it was mistaken. In fact, this sense of our immediate mood being the real one is illusory and the reverse is true: our sense of reality is dependent upon our mood; we are the creatures of our moods.

Although moods are not permanent, habitually depressed moods become subjects for clinical treatment. The sufferer may be agitated or withdrawn and apathetic, suicidally acting on a sudden impulse or a meticulous plan. There is also the possibility of a dangerous state of self-neglect.

Art as therapy is one means of alleviating this suffering if the setting is dedicated to creative art. Many patients can withdraw safely and begin to recover behind drawing boards, using their art work to accompany them on the journey back to mental health. Wordless insights can result from splashes, scribbles or delicate explorations in paint or clay if sufficient space and time is given and the therapist can follow the patient's symbolic images.

In claiming art as a therapeutic vehicle for depressed patients I do not forget that they may be prescribed other forms of treatment as well. However, these treatments have not cured a patient who is recommended for art therapy. The necessary change of attitude can only be made within the individual patient and depends on the positive use that he or she makes of innate creative initiative.

ART THERAPY IN PATIENT GROUPS

Art therapy for a depressed individual may have to be conducted in an open hospital group, where doctors and nurses have access. These conditions cannot, I think, be seen in terms of a group psychotherapy that requires a period of close relationship with other members and undisturbed sessions with a therapist.

If depression becomes pervasive as an illness, the flexible balance between different moods and attitudes to life is disturbed. Some people seem fixed in acute unhappiness while others seem frozen in immaculate indifference to everything or succumb to a state of helpless, psycho-physical inertia.

DEPRESSION AND SUICIDE

Art therapists are aware of an association of prolonged depression with suicide, which may not be their responsibility when a patient is in hospital but is an important concern when working with those who attend as out-patients. I am in no position to make a general statement, but in my own work I have not seen a depressed patient reacting with despair if he or she has become deeply absorbed in creating art that is offered as therapeutic containment in regular sessions. Only two instances come close; one patient was unable to interest herself in drawing and rejected art therapy after the first session (Simon 1991: 151) and another, Jean, I shall describe in detail.

People who succumb to agitated depression advertise their despair, and consequently they usually get help. The suffering of those whose depression withdraws them from life in a sort of inertia is less easy to detect. Others, who appear actively hostile to life, may come too late for help; they are adept at undermining sympathy. This third type demands our closest attention.

THE TRADITIONAL TRANSITION IN DEPRESSED PATIENT'S ART

An individual who is suffering from severe depression may not appear to be particularly unhappy but rather coldly self-sufficient. If they are persuaded to use an art material they usually draw, making small, conventional images and show no satisfaction in the art material or the object created. The work is skilful, but if they complete a sketch they do so as an allotted task. They are frustrating people who often arouse hostility or indifference.

Winnicott has described the tragic aridity of this illness, which he associates with an attitude of compliance:

> the world and its details being recognized but only as something to be fitted in with or demanding adaptation. Compliance carries with it a sense of futility for the individual and is associated with the idea that nothing matters and that life is not worth living.
>
> (Winnicott 1971: 65)

The style of art associated with such a habitual state of mind is Traditional, showing an overlap between Massive and Linear styles. This results in an art form that is both perceptive and thoughtful, but which is sadly lacking in intuitive feeling and empathy. The patient's attitude is impersonal, factual or abrasive. The art work is usually minimal, lacking colour or any sense of emotional commitment. This style is rarely used consistently in clinically depressed patients because, unless forced to attend, such a patient would not paint at all.

As a modification of the Traditional Massive style in depressive art the clarity and formality of the shapes and forms is immediately apparent. Images are presented factually or conventionally idealized, representing the surface of external appearances. Winnicott described this aspect of defence:

> The resolution of the paralysing depression came each day when at last it was time to get up and, at the end of her ablutions and dressing she could 'put on her face'. Now she felt rehabilitated and could meet the world.
>
> (Winnicott 1971: 114)

The art form is a make-up, providing definition to blurred outlines, faint tints and vague shapes. Its superficiality makes it a particularly precarious style in therapy, for the effect of normality could contribute to an illusion that lasting therapeutic benefit had occurred.

I will describe the progress of two women attending group art therapy, one an out-patient, suffering from depression and exhaustion, and an in-patient who seemed at first to be mad with anxiety and despair.

JEAN

I have written about this young woman in greater detail in *The Symbolism of Style* (1991: 151–5). Jean was a pale, pretty, childlike young woman who was asthmatic and habitually depressed by her inability to care for her husband and children as fully as she wished. On her first visit her timid passivity made her difficult to contact in the busy art group and she seemed content to sit quietly with folded hands. She had brought some neat little watercolour copies of flower paintings to show me, and when she spoke about herself she did not complain of depression but of asthma and her difficulty in getting a drug that was strong enough to control her breathing, yet not so strong that it made her ill.

At my suggestion she moved from her seat by the wall and chose a place at a large table that was laden with art materials, choosing small brushes and thin paint to make some little sketches of flowers from memory. These faintly coloured drawings were spread about a sheet of white paper, like little posies a child might pick, put down and forget.

The sketches that Jean brought were made in a transitional style of Traditional art, pretty, conventional images, dexterously painted. When I had time to sit with her for a few minutes she talked readily but breathlessly about her asthma and went on to mention the ease she had found once, when sitting in a church garden, talking to a cat.

I suggested that she might like to retain this memory by painting a view of it and, over some weeks, Jean developed this painting in the Traditional Massive style, showing herself as a tiny dot, as if seen from above, sitting on the garden bench. The cat was clearly represented and Jean's footsteps in the snow were very much larger than her self-representation. As the painting progressed, the style regressed slightly when she overpainted the church in darker tones, 'to show its strength', she said.

This style of Massive transition intensified the emotional effect of her picture, reducing the sense of space so that the church looked much nearer than it had originally appeared to be (Plate 12).

Jean had become more animated and I felt very hopeful that she could find a way out of her depression. She seemed quietly settled in the group and expressed pleasure in painting, adding that it helped her breathing. It seemed as if the painting was symbolizing a renewed hope of living an active and emotionally fulfilling life, closely in touch with a tangible world that had been escaping her in her depression. Indeed, it seemed as if painting this world might be a way of reconciling her inner and outer needs.

The content of Jean's picture is full of self-images in various moods: the open gates, the cat that sits by itself, the circular, empty flower bed cleared for the winter and the strange effect of the bench where Jean had sat. Painted from the aerial view, it looked ambiguous, and Jean had shown her footsteps encircling it. There was also a small dark cloud in the sky, carefully worked over and seeming to be full of meaning.

Jean continued working on this painting for several sessions until she had to stay at home for some weeks to nurse her sick children. On the week that she returned to the art group I was ill and the session was held in my absence by a nurse, who noticed how exhausted and depressed Jean seemed. She started to paint a swan on a narrow stream (Figure 6.1) but did not finish it. Before the next session I was told that Jean had accidentally taken a fatal overdose.

Jean had only attended for a few sessions and most of these were spent in painting the churchyard scene. She described the church as 'strong and powerful' and had spoken of the 'beautiful' coloured glass windows of angels. She was particularly pleased with her painting of the heavy church buttresses and the notice-board.

Although Jean was attending day hospital for depression she was not considered to be suicidal. Her death seemed an accident – an accident that should not have occurred had her drug intake been supervised. But

Figure 6.1 The Swan, Traditional transition

was there any evidence in her pictures to suggest that she might have contemplated taking her life?

When we turn to the message of Jean's art styles there was a dramatic change from a Traditional style of pallid, idealized drawings of flowers to the Massive effect of the landscape. Within a single picture Jean's mood had moved from the perceptive towards emotional expression shown in overpainting and darkening the colours, particularly the red brick church, and adding bright colour to the windows, as if they were lit from inside. This alteration had the effect of foreshortening the perspective to make it look up-ended, drawing background and foreground together. The details of its naturalism invite the viewer to study this painting.

The style of Jean's final picture reverted to that of her little flower paintings, a Traditional transition that showed the swan neatly, thus absolving the viewer from any need to contemplate the scene.

From her art style rather than her behaviour during her stay in the group I could see that Jean's attitude to life had changed very quickly indeed. The symbolism of the church garden included a Circle of Self well established in the centre of the picture, ringed round with bushes and a grass verge prepared for new growth in the spring. This symbol as an image of assertiveness was negative, nothing was growing inside but the ground had been prepared. I saw it as predictive rather than actual, but had thought that she would make many more paintings of the outer world before her sense of self could achieve this potential and fully integrate inner and outer reality.

Most sadly, this creative initiative was interrupted by her children's need and when she came back to the open situation of the art group Jean was not able to return to her self-assuring mood. Her final painting has much of the lifeless factualism of the Traditional Linear style – its flatness, the horizontal division of the areas and lack of recession. The perfection of the solitary swan and the leafless trees poignantly illustrate her emotional withdrawal.

Art therapy does not operate in limbo; other factors are involved, other people, doctors, nurses, family and friends. Jean had not indicated that her life was not worth living and I did not know any details of her day-to-day life. Family and friends hope or expect that psychiatric help will restore a patient to the way he or she was before the breakdown, but recovery entails change as the inevitable outcome of conflict between the wish to be well and the wish to stay the same.

Before going further into the positive and negative aspects of art subjects and styles I will give some excerpts from art therapy with Dora, who was suffering from depression in a very different way.

DORA

Dora was an in-patient in a psychiatric hospital where my work was limited to one, two-hour weekly group session. It might seem that someone as distressed as Dora could expect little help from such an apparently superficial contact, but that would be to ignore the fact that, as Jean had shown us, it does not take much time to reach creative initiative when a provision can be found by a patient who is ready to use it. Although I shall concentrate on the content and style of Dora's painting, this is not to say that the sessions were altogether without words, although at first her confusion made any verbal communication impossible.

Dora seemed distraught when first brought to the art room by a nurse, who sat with her throughout the session. Dora was a middle-aged woman who managed to look dishevelled in spite of the nurse's best efforts. Weeping almost continuously about the horror of cockroaches swarming over her kitchen floor all night, it seemed unlikely that she would be able to attend to anything else, yet, when directed by the nurse she took a sheet of card from a pile of papers and a palette of bright gouache colours, and sat down at a small table where she started to paint straight away (Figure 6.2).

Figure 6.2 House-face, Archaic Linear to Archaic transition

Dora had a large brush and made broad diagonal lines from the top left-hand corner of the paper. I was very surprised to see her work so decisively for, in spite of considerable agitation, her drawing was unhesitating and clear and it seemed that she remembered some past instruction to wash the brush between each colour as she filled some of the spaces.

The nurse became anxious when Dora suddenly got up, but she had gone to fetch a smaller brush. Although colour was used mainly in flat areas and lines there was one exception, a vomit-like mass of blackish brown, issuing from the mouth of a face she added to a square 'house' shape. Another face was drawn in a triangular shape above this 'house-face' and Dora continued painting to the lower right-hand corner where she drew a red-haired object, a doll or a helpless child, from whose lap ascended a snake. Finally, she drew three small red shapes like insects, attached to claw-like lines. By the end she was weeping and moaning as she worked. My eyes swept over the separate parts of this painting in an effort to sum up its meaning, but the impression gave me no consistent subject, only my guesses were noted. Unless Dora could tell me the meaning of House-face's hints, her meaning lay only in the style, the way that the shapes and colours were made.

Frances Tustin refers to special difficulties in interpreting non-verbal communications:

It will be obvious that in such a situation, where there is a paucity of verbal associations, other details have to be used as evidence for interpretations which are deduced from different, and in some cases more slender evidence than that available when the patient is more verbally communicative. . . . One difficulty in dealing with early material in this way is that an attempt has to be made to reconstruct, through the sophisticated medium of words, a play of affect first experienced at the preverbal stage of development.

(Tustin 1986: 243)

This problem was also faced by Melanie Klein, Balint and many other psychoanalysts. As an art therapist I have another way of looking at the patient's wordless behaviour when it is applied to an art material. Only by this means can I see if there is any need to intervene or to put into words what I think is going on.

Tustin explores the difficulty that is inherent in the therapist's need to communicate the virtually incommunicable:

Non-verbal material has to be used and concepts have to be found for un-conceptualized material. It is difficult to be sure that what one is seeing is not idiosyncratic to oneself alone. Thus confirmation of one's findings from workers using different approaches from one's own is reassuring and necessary.

(Tustin 1990: 77–8)

Creative art symbolizes the mental activity that Freud called 'visual thinking' and ascribed to a primitive process of fantasy in which the artist/patient allows images to enact meaning that Tustin calls 'a play of affect' (1986: 125). As Tustin implies, then, a therapist's attention can be directed to behaviour that normally escapes attention when we are listening to what is being said. In the absence of a clear 'message' in Dora's picture, I needed to understand its style as far as I could.

The scale of Dora's painting is Archaic and its diagonality places it in the area of transition, somewhere between Linear and Massive art – even though the only Massive image is in the vomit-like brownish shape coming from the square face and the suggestion of solidity in the little figure in the bottom right-hand corner. The Archaic Linear dominance of the style implies a mood that is flooded by violent sensuous experience.

We are normally so far from ongoing consciousness of our sensuous existence that it is hard for us to understand images or other expressions of its reality unless these are associated with a change, such as illness, sexual excitement or the shuddering of fear. Dora's continuing experience of the flesh-creeping horror of cockroaches seemed incomprehensible to those around her, but her second painting (Figure 6.3) shows her sensuous revulsion in the proliferation of insects that reflect the trauma continuing on her skin. This painting covers the whole paper, giving an effect of an entangling skein of sensation.

Although Dora's mood was fearfully disturbed, her painting was not chaotic; the shapes were clearly defined and in spite of her distress she seemed to know what she was doing, although it was not clear that she knew why.

I think Jung understood this state, which he ascribed to the creative process in artists as well as patients:

> We would do well, therefore to think of the creative process as a living thing implanted in the human psyche. ... Depending on its energy charge, it may appear either as a mere disturbance of conscious activities or as a supraordinate authority which can harness the ego to its purpose.
>
> (Jung 1993: 75)

Jung called this 'living thing' the collective unconscious and, without straying far from Dora's individual drawings of snakes on trees, this symbol occurs in many paintings by patients in therapy and others (Simon 1991: 103–7). I was inclined to think of the serpent in the Garden of Eden and its association with the Tree of Knowledge, but such speculations would lead us away from Dora herself.

As Dora continued to paint conglomerations of insects and snakes mixed with tree-like, entangling lines (Figure 6.3) she spoke constantly of

Figure 6.3 Snakes and Insects, Archaic transition

Figure 6.4 The Yellow Background, Archaic to Massive transition

the horror that these creatures aroused, and her tears, falling unheeded down her face, gave the effect of desperate but uncomprehended grief, yet it seemed that painting was really life-saving, as she said it was.

I was not told what other means of help were available to her but eventually Dora became less agitated. Figure 6.4 seems to be a turning point, for she methodically covered white paper with yellow paint and had to wait patiently for it to dry before she could add a rootless young tree and two highly decorated snakes, their snouts cut off by the edge of the paper. A third, smaller snake is shown with its snout placed close to the silhouette of a huge cockroach. This snake was meticulously painted; dry colour has been carefully pressed on to the surface while it was wet and this suggests that Doris's agitation was passing and she was able to represent her images with some attention to the space they occupied. As a result, the Archaic Massive effect of the snakes is modified and Dora seems to be edging her fantasy towards Massive transitional representation, in which ambivalent feelings are often shown by magical or metamorphic images.

Dora stopped crying in the art room, but still painted energetically and confidently, using large and small brushes with thick paint. The next development shows that she could envisage a consistent theme. A huge snake is lying diagonally across a grassy plot, its head turned back to face a Massive cockroach that appears to scamper out of the top edge of the paper. The snake's tail encircles a dark area that suggests its emergence from a depression in the ground (Figure 6.5).

Figure 6.5 Snake in the Grass, Archaic Massive

I will describe the next example (Figure 6.6) in some detail in order to illustrate the flexibility of Dora's creative initiative. The painting began as a sea of wavy lines cascading over the whole area of the card she had chosen. When she had painted this to her satisfaction she added a large yellow Circle in the centre that looked like the sun in the sky, but then she covered this disc with brown paint and green, grass-like strokes, suggesting an island, bisected diagonally by a thick black strip that she widened at the lower edge, as if it was a road, then adding tentacle-like shapes to the upper end. This changed its effect to be more like a huge insect. Then Dora painted these shapes and made them into leaves by overpainting green with yellow spots. Finally she added the climbing snake.

I see an important difference here between her earlier, 'piecemeal' painting, in which it seems that many images were used as symbolic equivalents for Dora's kinaesthetic sensations, and the island painting, in which it seemed that she had found a symbolic image of the Self in which the snake could be contained.

Dora seemed ready now to look at the actual nature of the traumatic experience that had precipitated her breakdown, and when she was considered ready to be discharged from hospital her need to appreciate the difference between inner and outer reality was truly challenged.

Although attendance as an out-patient necessitated some awkward travelling, Dora continued with art therapy and Plate 13 is the first painting

Figure 6.6 An Island, Massive transition

she made in her new situation. It shows a rainy pavement. Depression is implied by its pale watery tones of blue and grey, filling the lower half of the paper with a flat pattern of paving stones that look like a wall. The upper half of the painting is shown as a wind-swept sky where a huge half moon lies on its back. The upper part of the picture is in an Archaic Massive style and the lower in Archaic Linear, symmetrical and static, where even the raindrops fall, like tears, in the geometric spaces of the paving stones. The picture looks as if it is weighing the life-lessness of despair against the vitality of madness, a visual metaphor for manic-depressive psychosis, the pavement like a wall that cuts off all sight of life except for the sky and its moon as a symbol of lunacy. The painting clearly showed me how very hard it was for Dora to move from the shelter of hospital life, with its securities and limitations, and go out to the everyday world of hard pavements and passive, teardrop rain.

Dora was able to survive and continue with art therapy as an out-patient. Her eventual recovery was symbolized as a landscape that reached a limited illusion of space as a field, painted in recession until it met the soil of the orchard where the spatial relation breaks down into the effect of a vertical background with trees arranged in tiers, like the painted back-cloth of a stage, too brilliant in colour and size to be faded into the cool shades needed to create an illusion of distance. It looks as if Dora strug-gled to show recession to the horizon but failed to get beyond the trees, leaving a misty mess of washed-out colours on the right (Figure 6.7).

Figure 6.7 Yellow Orchard, Massive transition to Traditional

Dora did spontaneously achieve consistent recession in her final painting (Figure 6.8). The Traditional Massive element in this landscape has dominated the Massive transition, merging a rough, Archaic quality of direct, energetic painting with consistent spatial illusion. I see in this painting a style of symbolic relation between Self and Other that psychosis had, for a time denied her. Her appreciation of interdependence in affective life is symbolized in the shadows falling from the trees.

Figure 6.8 Fields in the Sun, Traditional Massive

THREE TYPES OF DEPRESSION

Depression is usually considered to fall into one of three categories: reactive, endogenous and psychotic. In Chapter 7 I describe the reactive depression that is precipitated by bereavement. Here, I think that the depression suffered by Jean could be described as endogenous and Dora's agitated depression as psychotic.

Endogenous depression, supposedly innate to a patient's outlook, can perhaps be seen as a pathological version of the Kleinian 'depressive position' occurring in people who show an intuitive/perceptive style of Traditional Massive art if they become mentally ill. These patients suffer from an exaggerated sense of guilt and are overwhelmed by their responsibilities. Their own needs seem extinguished and this leaves them open to a self-neglect that might be fatal, not usually through positive self-destruction but simply through abandonment of the Self.

Dora's agitation and grief generated an active response which was easily channelled into creative work that led her towards recovery, for, if a patient initiates her own art, without more help than is given by the therapist's concerned attention, her attitude will change as creative initiative arouses self-esteem.

If we accept that an habitual style of art reflects the patient's attitude to life and that this attitude, though not in itself pathological, has contributed to the illness, then any change in that style, however small, is to be welcomed as an opportunity to experience life from a different point of view.

In the example of a patient I called John (Simon 1991: 118–25), being regularly occupied with painting had a beneficial effect upon his restless anxiety and this improved his chance of recovery from pulmonary tuberculosis, and the style and content of his painting demonstrated the way in which painting enabled his attitude to change.

We need much more understanding of psychosomatic interrelation if we are better to understand and support the beneficent effects of creative arts upon the whole individual and the individual's attitude towards reality. We need to understand more of what is taking place in the deep and unconscious part of the patient's mind, operating psycho-physically before conscious intentions and repressed thoughts might be discovered in the content. If we can comprehend the significance of the postures and gestures that make painting and sculpture, drama and play, we will be more effective and less interfering, ensuring that healing is not delayed, 'scabbed over' or blocked.

At present, symbolic images, like 'witch-balls' reflect all forms of interpretation that are presented to them, and only by their habitual style can we recognize the way a patient imagines, and the limitations that this way imposes.

THREE STYLES OF ART IN DEPRESSED PATIENTS

Art styles used by patients with a depressive illness are constellated around the Traditional Massive style associated with an intuitive grasp of external reality; the effects of interrelation create the familiar appearance of this style, pervading light and shade affecting all surfaces, colours and tones. Without knowing the precise distance between two objects, we come in childhood to grasp intuitively the fact of objects being nearer or further away. If our sight and intelligence is normal we see objects related in space, but this is not necessarily an apperception. We see objects three-dimensionally in space but may be able to represent them like this only occasionally, or not at all. An artist who habitually paints landscape as if the picture were a cone down which we can peer to the horizon may be quite unable to achieve this effect if conscious thought is involved, since in effect the process of thought may separate the meaning of objects from their appearance. This change of attitude can create truly enormous difficulties for an artist, and these are only partially resolved by rules of geometric perspective.

Perceptual memory enables us to grasp relations between subject and subject as well as the effect of objects on each other. Once we are able to enjoy the look of things that we cannot reach we are able to distance ourselves to some extent from the immediacy of passions, to anticipate some things intuitively and to appreciate restraint.

Possibly a reader will be inclined to associate this attitude with the positive result of the Oedipal crisis, especially as most of us acquire the ability to depict space in the middle years of childhood; but these virtues are bought at the cost of some inhibition of natural possessiveness and assertiveness.

An intuitive individual who becomes depressed may show withdrawal from external reality by the effect of blurring and fuzziness in his painting. Spatial relations, shown by tones and colours, suffer in this way, and apathy affects the artist's creative initiative. If therapeutic conditions can be established and maintained the work will change, either through the clarifying of boundaries and greater emphasis on local colour and tonal contrasts, as in a Traditional transition, or through change to a larger, coarser style, suggesting the vigour of a Massive transition towards Archaic art.

At first, Jean's art was an example of an anti-clockwise movement from the Traditional transition to a Massive tradition. She had been adept at painting Christmas or birthday cards but in the uncritical atmosphere of the art group, surrounded by patients using paints in many different styles, she slipped easily into Traditional naturalism and further back towards emotional expression of her need for support. I had hoped that she could have found this inner strength in herself, but there was no time for this to develop.

Dora's art developed beyond the Archaic Massive style shown in 'Snake in the Grass' (Figure 6.5). Her later paintings include elements of space and other naturalistic imagery. Such recollections may confront idealization and suffer the limitations of vague notions, symbolized as boundary lines that limit habitual associations or indicate repressed material. I asked Dora if she had enjoyed painting and she said that she had not, as she had been 'so bad at it at school'.

POSITIVE AND NEGATIVE ASPECTS OF THE PATIENTS' STYLES

Each style symbolizes an attitude that has a positive and negative aspect. The basic Traditional Massive style is an appreciation of relation and sameness but also represents the dethroning of the omnipotent Self, the introduction of guilt and reparation.

The Archaic transition is both a release of emotion and playfulness yet also regression into a quasi-magical world where external reality can be contaminated by projections of atavistic emotion; a nightmare world, haunted by grotesque, anthropomorphic images that threaten at any moment to turn into something else. Archaic transitional art combines sensuous and emotional realities that have come into conflict due to immaturity or some form of mental or physical illness. A therapeutic progression or maturational process shows in massive overpainting of the flat, linear shapes, while regression is seen when solid-looking forms appear flattened by emphatic outlines.

THE CONCEPT OF WHOLENESS

The concept of a whole Self suggests that we are capable of experiencing the reality of inner and outer life to an equal extent, yet if it were possible to do so we should be divided by the impossibility of choice. Of course this is not the case; we all have limitations that prevent us from thinking at times when we are emotionally involved, or feeling when we are thinking, or responding intuitively when we are overtaken by sensuous reality, or grasping the reality of our senses when we are intuitively absorbed in that which is other than our Self. The four basic aspects of reality are available to us, although they cannot be held in consciousness at the same time.

JEAN'S ART STYLES

Jean brought to therapy the positive aspect of a Traditional style that shaped her delicate drawings. Her skill reassured herself and others, illustrating an ideal world where she could be a perfect wife and mother.

When this ideal was attacked by her physical disability her sketches became empty clichés and she became depressed. Perhaps she suffered suicidal thoughts that further harmed her self-esteem.

When her creative initiative was released through therapeutic use of art she was able to make a benign regression to a typically non-judgemental, Traditional Massive style, and here she found time to remember her rest in the church garden. This recollection allowed her art to regress further to a Massive transition, and she repainted the church to show its strength.

We might see in this fantasy that Jean shed her defence of being a skilful amateur artist and invalid wife and mother, responding to another part of herself that was emotionally exhausted and needed to play with her painting in a rather childlike way and, in the metaphor of her imagery, be a child of the Father.

At this point, when she was most vulnerable to her emotional needs, she was called upon by her children's illness to forget herself and attend exclusively to others. I should imagine that a sadistic superego asserted itself against her physical and emotional needs, either leading to her failure to protect herself from its attack, or leading her to reject life altogether. Her despair was shown in a revision to a style of Traditional transition in its negative aspect, where neither perceptual memories nor factual reality supported her.

DORA'S ART STYLES

It may be that Dora's psychotic behaviour preserved her from suicide, although there had been some sort of a suicidal gesture. By openly demonstrating the suffering that was hidden in Jean's asthma, Dora's breakdown could be cared for and she could be given enough time to work through her depression. From the start of her art therapy Dora showed a positive appreciation of the opportunity for self-expression when, for instance, she carefully cleaned her brush at a time when, otherwise, she seemed extremely confused.

Dora's first painting was dominated by an Archaic Linear style of sensuous reality, only slightly relieved by one Archaic Massive area. The next stage seemed to be a consistent use of Massive transitional painting that lasted some months. This only began to change at the time of Figure 6.4, when a new (to me) display of patience and intricate elaboration of the reptiles seemed to show ambivalence towards the part of her life that they symbolized.

The huge scale of Archaic dominance continued until it was modified in Massive transitions, such as the island, that seemed to symbolize her capacity to contain, if not resolve, the traumatic experience associated with the snake symbol. After that, Dora was able to leave the hospital and cope with the everyday world.

The Archaic Massive style of her first painting as an out-patient symbolized the split she found in reality at a time when it seemed separated into
desperately cold, rainy pavements and a mad but lively existence in a
limitless sky and lunatic moon – symbol of her incomplete Circle of Self.
Was it Dora's art imagery that guided her psychic integration or some
other benign circumstance of this time?

My common sense tells me that none can go alone through life without
being influenced by its circumstances; nevertheless, it is equally clear that
it is how we use circumstance that makes the difference between happi-
ness and unhappiness, madness and sanity.

After Dora had made this critical image her art style developed steadily
towards the Traditional Massive, first giving an impression of limited space
that I describe as arranged like a stage and backdrop – as if space was
bent up at right angles from the foreground. After this she painted many
landscapes of the countryside in this style, until it subtly changed once
more to extend the illusion of distance by related tones and colours, which
were used weave a consistent space to a horizon.

This growing sense of spatial relation between parts is exemplified by
Dora's use of shadows as shown in Figure 6.8.

SUMMARY

No art style is itself pathological, but rather the style presents an image
of the artist's state of mind. Anyone suffering from habitual depression
reflects the particular quality of this state as he or she paints by one of
three styles, each showing positive and negative values in the attitude it
unconsciously reflects. Paintings by Jean and Dora, two patients using art
as a therapy, show how these styles were used.

Jean seemed to find herself in the symbolism of a Massive transitional
style, expressing her need for emotional commitment to external reality.
She was not seen to require the protective care implied by in-patient status
that would have given her the time and place to work through this need.

Dora's first painting style shows her mood preoccupied by a traumatic
sensuous experience that was soon relocated in an habitual attitude of
agitated depression symbolized by a transitional style between Archaic
and Traditional art. Paintings such as these appear to contain mood-swings
between the demands of inner and outer reality. Over months in a psychiatric hospital these fluctuations became centred on her need for symbolic
integration, finally achieved in a Traditional Massive style of landscape
painting.

REFERENCES

Jung, C. G. (1993) *The Spirit in Man, Art and Literature*, London: Ark.
Simon, R. M. (1991) *The Symbolism of Style*, London: Routledge.
Tustin, F. (1986) *Autistic Barriers in Neurotic Patients*, London: Karnac Books.
—— (1990) *The Protective Shell in Children and Adults*, London: Karnac Books.
Winnicott, D. W. (1971) *Playing and Reality*, London: Tavistock.

Chapter 7

Bereavement and dying in art therapy

You and I must surely die.
Death does not cheat or lie
So why should I?

(A verse from a patient's poem)

Physical death is a simple fact, complicated by our lack of practical experience. Although we may see other people die we cannot know what it is for them.

Because we don't know how death is experienced we invent hypotheses that are inevitably limited by our own way of seeing things. Freud, for instance – perhaps because he constantly engaged in the life-and-death struggle of his creative genius – saw death as the end of a life-long conflict between the instinct to survive and the instinct to succumb. Winnicott was concerned with psychological death as the loss of creative apperception that makes life worth living. I also consider that the quality of life is the deciding factor in anticipating death – can I manage a good enough death, something more than failure to stay alive? How can I help anyone else to work through bereavement and find life worth living?

In the dictionary definition, to bereave is 'to rob, deprive and leave desolate', and I distinguish bereavement from death because not all deaths cause the pain of bereavement, nor are all bereavements caused by death. I find that all who need psychological help from art at some stage discover in their art a place for feelings of being bereft; they may have lived for years without remembering the loss and perhaps have been forced to displace their sense of desolation. Others, adults or children, have always been unable to forget and suffer a sense of unending deprivation.

In this chapter I give instances of different ways in which some people used creative art to work through the pain and fear of being bereft of life. But first I need to indicate one way in which creativity can fail to be seen as a working space for bereavement.

ANN

> [We all need] the common pool of humanity, into which individuals
> and groups of people may contribute, and from which we may all draw
> *if we have somewhere to put what we find.*
>
> (Winnicott 1971: 99; emphasis in original)

Ann had been widowed and her friends tried to help her forget her grief
and join them for art classes. She was known to be artistic and good with
her hands so she decided to try clay modelling. She began to make the
conventional figurine of a Victorian lady, skilfully managing details of the
delicate, petal-like flounces of a crinoline. Her friends noticed that this
gave the figure an effect of advanced pregnancy and it caused some good-
humoured chaff, so Ann cut away the front of the skirt quite drastically
and continued to work on her model, but then it came to look like a
rugged old country woman (Figure 7.1).

Although the group admired this transformation and encouraged her
to complete it, Ann could only feel that it showed her lack of skill. She
was adamant that she had lost her talent; she abandoned the model and
did not return to the class.

Ann's reaction demonstrates the importance of having 'somewhere to put
what we find' when an intention to forget is threatened by an unconscious
compulsion to recollect. The threatened awareness of bereavement was
intolerable when she and her friends had connived to forget. Ann's creative
impulse showed her need to give symbolic form to ways she had been bereft.

In the casual atmosphere of the art group she could not grasp and use
the positive aspect of the symbolic images she had created. Pregnancy is
an anticipation of new life and old age is its completion, but Ann saw the
images as failures of her will to maintain a conventional stereotype: her
destructiveness showed the anger and anxiety that threatens us when
emotion has no outlet and must be denied.

In the next case good medical care was given that included concerned
attention to patients' emotional needs.

JOYCE

Joyce was a middle-aged woman who was recommended for art therapy.
Terminal disease was rapidly closing her life, and when I visited she was
confined to bed. At first she was not interested in the idea of painting:
everything seemed too difficult in her weakened state and also she was
afraid that her lack of skill could not be hidden from anyone who came
in while she was painting.

When these obstacles had been cleared away she still found it impossible to complete a picture. Like Ann, as soon as her work deviated from
her intention in the slightest way she could neither follow the fantasy nor

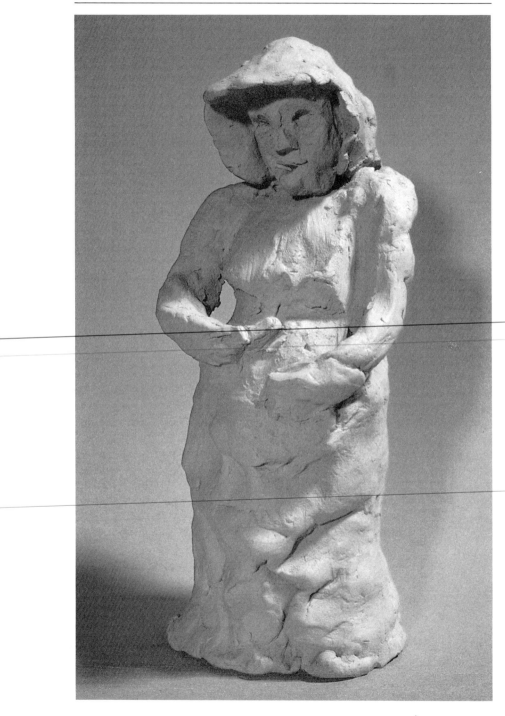

Figure 7.1 The Old Woman, Traditional Massive

correct it. It seemed as if she tried to put a desperate need for perfect control into every brush stroke. Marion Milner helps us to understand this resistance to freely creative art:

> I noticed that the effort needed in order to see the edges of objects as they really look, stirred a dim fear, a fear of what might happen if one let go one's mental hold on the outline which kept everything separate and in its place; and it was similar to that fear of a wide focus of attention that I had noticed in earlier experiments.
>
> (Milner 1986: 31)

Joyce's resistance to the free play of imagination was physically and emotionally exhausting for both of us and sometimes I felt that her efforts were self-destructive. However, her doctors thought that there was some benefit in my weekly visits and they encouraged me to continue.

She was bitter, blaming me for failing to help her, imagining that I withheld some technique that would solve her difficulties, but she could not use practical help; it was as if she was determined to fail. She asked for a ruler but did not hold it steady or allow me to hold it for her; colours that she intended to be delicately bright became harsh under her brush. Moreover, her actual weakness created many real problems that entangled with those that she imposed on herself. Especially frustrating was her idealization of nature; she felt that she could never do justice to the beauty of the trees and flowers that seemed to her the only proper material of art. Time and again she tried to paint her idea of a garden 'that would be paradise to live in'. Figure 7.2 shows one of her many failed attempts to create this perfection. The work is typical of the Traditional Linear style, an art form that is planned and consciously controlled.

On one of my weekly visits she mentioned a strange and fascinating dream. She remembered it as the view of a fountain set in the sea that she could glimpse through the bars of some tall gates. Although she considered the image illogical, I was glad to see that she could describe something of her own with pleasure and I suggested that she might like to paint this vivid scene. On my next visit I found that she had been working away at her vision and she continued to work on it for a number of weeks (Plate 14).

This was the first picture she had been able to continue and complete. I was particularly pleased when she told me that she had lowered the gates 'because they obstructed the view'. Like Ann's image of the country woman, Joyce's painting developed in a Massive transitional style. Although this style has a primitive and rather clumsy appearance, Joyce did not criticize it nor did she seem to notice that the colours were quite dark and the lines were not perfectly straight. She developed the Massive effect by overpainting, and this satisfied her need for tactile realism –

Figure 7.2 Paradise Garden, Traditional Linear

she was delighted by the effects of weight and solid form that appeared effortlessly from under her brush.

When at last the painting seemed finished she had another vivid dream, this time of two dogs gambolling on a shady lawn before a little temple. She painted this rather quickly and called it *The Happy Hunting Ground* (Plate 15).

Both paintings continued to absorb her attention and when she became too weak to sit up she continued to study them, sometimes adding a few touches from her prone position. She kept the paintings within reach, convinced that they were visions of her life to come.

Joyce's change of attitude was reflected in her art styles. Her original demand for perfect control had limited her to the Traditional Linear style that illustrated her unremitting efforts to avoid thinking about the helplessness of dying. She was miraculously released from this by her deeply satisfying dream: then she could paint effortlessly in the Massive transitional style. As Joyce worked on this image she found the creative freedom that had eluded her. Released from the idealism of a Traditional art style, her love of life was given a form in which the after-life was included as its continuity. Painting transformed her dreams into symbolic images that she used to come with confidence to the end of her life.

Figure 7.3 The Third Eye, Massive transition

My work with Joyce gave me a glimpse of the destructive force of bereavement if it is turned against itself in anger and despair.

BARBARA

Barbara was a young woman who had become almost totally blind and disabled by diabetes. She found these increasing infirmities intolerable but eagerly responded to the opportunity to model in clay. She first made a little oblong box from five pieces of flattened clay, then added a lid to close it. I asked Barbara what she would like to put inside and she replied: 'Nothing. It's like my life: I'm boxed in. I can do nothing by myself any more. I'm not even allowed to walk down the garden path alone.'

As she was speaking she was handling another piece of clay, rolling it into a ball and squeezing it in her fingers, indenting its surface. I said that I could see that she was making something and asked her to feel what it might be. She said 'It's a head, but it has three eyes.' As she began to crush the clay I asked her to wait a little and consider the shape as it was, the shape her hand had made. Then she said: 'Perhaps it has the eye of wisdom.'

She continued to work on the head, drawing out the nose, shaping the eyes in their sockets and modelling a wide mouth half closed over teeth. As she developed the Massive forms of bony cheeks and jaw she spoke with pride of her dead father and her secure and happy childhood in his care (Figure 7.3).

Barbara was heartened by her modelling of the head and in the next session she began work on a skull, using the same technique of squeezed and indented clay. When the second model was completed there was a remarkable similarity in the two heads (Figure 7.4) although Barbara could see little of what she was doing. In making a skull she thought about the three indentations that had given her the idea of a head, but she did not give the skull a place for a third eye. Both models were Traditional in their naturalistic proportion but the mythic association in the first head suggested some Archaic association.

Barbara was almost elated by these works and enjoyed showing them to her doctor and gaining his admiration of the anatomical details. Then she spent some weeks modelling a foot and a hand to represent her disabilities for him; the models enabled her to contribute to his understanding and she could become a co-operative patient as well as showing her artistic skill.

JANE

Jane's art is an example of the predictive element in art that invites ideas formed through symbolic expression that could not be consciously

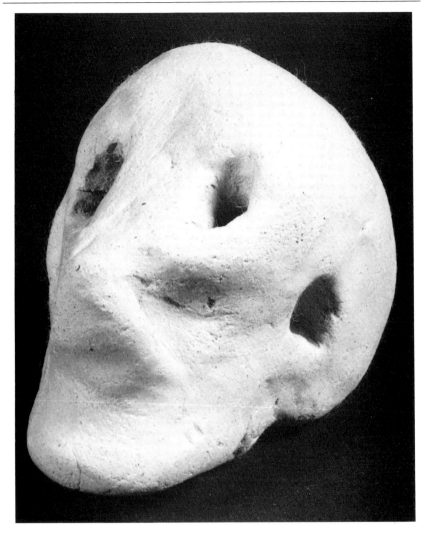

Figure 7.4 The Skull, Traditional transition

contained otherwise. Jane was seventy-eight and had been in hospital for three years, confined to a wheelchair. As a farmer's wife she had cared for her busy family and lived surrounded by animals; now her active mind was tied to the extremely limited hospital routine. Her doctor considered her clinically depressed but when she joined a small group of patients who wished to paint together she came eagerly, pleased to have a new environment for a couple of hours a week.

Figure 7.5 Home, Linear transition

Her doctor was pleased with the success of his suggestion, for she quickly recovered her interest in people and her previous initiative-taking attitude towards life, making efforts to wheel herself to the art room and to befriend patients who previously had sat silently beside her. She sometimes sang hymns as she painted and made humorous remarks about the farm animals she liked to draw.

Jane first drew with charcoal but soon realized that she preferred to work with felt-tipped pens (Figure 7.5), later adding flat areas of body colour to fill in the larger spaces (Figure 7.7).

At first her pictures were disorganized, but as she continued in the Traditional Linear style she organized the pictures in factual relation to the subject-matter, which became varied and often matched the light-hearted mood she expressed by writing on her work (Figure 7.6).

Jane's two-dimensional style continued over months of regular weekly attendance. As her pictures became more rationally organized Jane used flat washes of blue and green to indicate ground and sky (Figure 7.7). During this time she described one picture (Figure 7.7):

> I did draw a couple of horses and a few sheep also a dog on green pasture, but I did not give the poor animals justice, they are not at all very nice on the drawing as I am very fond of all kinds of animals. . . . I myself had some very good conversations with them and I warned them about crossing the road when they were parked on the street and

Figure 7.6 The Farm, Traditional Linear

they understood every word. . . . We all shed quite a lot of sorrowful tears when they got old and died.

Jane's liberation of spirit heartened those who attended her. Her recovery from depression had a positive effect upon her family, the staff and patients in her ward. She attended regularly, painted steadily, and although her art style did not change much, the subject-matter of her last paintings showed that she had turned to the inner reality of her life and reached an acceptance of its ending. Both her earliest pictures and the last two are made as a transition between the Archaic and Traditional Linear styles, with the important difference that the first paintings were fragmented and rather confused while the last ones were factually coherent and metaphorical.

The first of these is a careful representation of two cottages drawn in red outline below a strong horizon, painted blue and green. The left-hand, larger house has a blue roof, windows and door filled in with felt pen. A dormer window has been added, indicating that this house has attributes of a remembered home. The smaller house has roof, windows and door filled in with green; three Circles are outlined in red, two are door handles and the third is larger, the outline of a sun, set over the house on the left. All the Circles were added finally to the picture with felt pen. The green house has 'SOLD' written on it and the blue house, 'FOR SALE' (Figure 7.8).

Figure 7.7 Horse Field, Traditional transition

A month later Jane made what was to be her last painting (Figure 7.9), a terrace of cottages set in front of a larger building. Jane reverted to her earlier, X-ray painting in this picture and limited herself to black felt pen, with blue for the sky and clay colour for the building in the background.

Figure 7.8 For Sale, Traditional Linear

Figure 7.9 Cottages for Sale, Traditional Linear

Each cottage is linked with a horizontal line at the roof and, except for the left-hand one, a continuing base line.

Each house indicates the process of withdrawal from life; every dwelling has an occupant, except the one on the far right. The first house has three windows upstairs and down and a figure outside, with its head in the doorway; the second house has three windows upstairs and the little figure stands in the downstairs room, furnished with a table and chair. The third house has only one window and the figure is inside; the fourth house is smaller and the figure seems without arms, with a tiny body and long legs; the final house is without a figure at all.

The title, *Cottages for Sale*, is written outside the containing frame of a large building that illustrates the promise of Jesus – 'In My Father's house there are many mansions' (Figure 7.9).

MISS RINK

Miss Rink was an apparently healthy and contented old lady who was living in a residential home where art sessions been introduced as means of therapy for some depressed and disabled residents. I have already described Miss Rink's art in my previous book (Simon 1991) as an example of the Traditional Massive style.

Although she was profoundly deaf, when Miss Rink was invited to join the art group she readily took some pastels and made faint scrawls along

Figure 7.10 Seascape, Traditional Massive

the top of the paper, reminiscent of the scribbles that little children use to mimic handwriting before they have learnt to form the alphabet. These marks she worked over for several weeks and during this time she asked for paint because she thought the blue scrawls looked like clouds. As time went on she developed her picture as a seascape.

The subject was built up by adding complementary images, a light-ship and a destroyer, a lighthouse and a wreck. As the work progressed, little by little Miss Rink's art became more and more decisive; she had no difficulty in presenting objects in space and the cool colours and subtle forms she made gave an air of tranquillity to the implicit violence of the scene. She described creative art in similar, moderate terms; it was, she observed, 'very entertaining' and it obviously amused her.

Miss Rink's art of recollected perception reflected her logical view of external reality; this contained her creative impulse very well until she needed an image of inner meaning that could not be seen objectively, simply as the inevitable consequence of life, like the destroyer she painted to oppose the light-ship or the wreck that created the need for a light-house. One day she added some curved shapes to the sea, on the left side. She asked me to guess what they might be and eventually she explained that they showed the wake of a torpedo. Then she altered the distant cliffs to indicate the wreck that had been hit and was sinking fast.

One day, during her work on the misty part of the sky Miss Rink had painted a naturalistic sun, half hidden by delicate clouds and giving an impression of shining from left to right. She asked me if she had made it look too big and when I told her that she should make it the size she wanted she replied, 'Then I shall make it bigger.'

As Miss Rink had not asked for advice before, this remark drew my attention to the sun which, as she worked, became an Archaic Circle ringed with heavy rays, the symbolic Circle of Self as the solar disc, eternally dying and being reborn (Figure 7.10).

Although Miss Rink introduced the Archaic sun symbol into her Traditional, naturalistic painting she retained the whitish yellow of the original colour; this softened the un-naturalistic effect. I understand her altered style as reflecting a considerable change from the rational balance of opposites she had presented by the complementary images of preservation and destruction at sea.

Miss Rink did not live to paint another picture: she suddenly weakened and died two weeks later. It is not possible to say how far she was aware of her art as bereavement work, but when this fine old lady came to the end of her life I visited her, and she thanked me for coming.

PREVAILING MOOD

Art we describe as 'creative' and 'original' contains images of the artist's inner and outer reality. The inner reality we call subjective, or symbolic, while the external appearance of inner life we see as its objective or traditional aspect. The proportions of inner and outer are adjusted according to the artist's prevailing mood, as this inevitably shapes his or her art style.

So far, the patients I have described used versions of art styes that are in the commonly prevailing traditions of representation. Ann wanted to re-create the sentimental idea of the past, exemplified by the *Crinoline Lady*, and Joyce also wanted an idealized version of life in her *Paradise Garden*. Barbara was deeply concerned with the metaphysical world but her art shaped this concern in the naturalistic appearance of the Traditional Massive style. Jane presented her ideas through the conventional attributes of the animals, people and houses she wished to illustrate. Her ideas were formed and presented in Linear, almost diagrammatic shapes that I have described as in transition between the Linear concepts. In her Traditional Massive style Miss Rink drew from her perceptual memory with the same freedom that has guided artists during the last 300 years. Thus, all these women symbolized their sense of bereavement within the framework of their conscious experience.

Not all the art of our present culture is traditional, nor does it inevitably include elements of a traditional style that would link it to an idea. Archaic art may seem to conflict with the culture and it's unfamiliarity may arouse

Figure 7.11 Easter Island idol, Archaic Linear

hostility. Nevertheless, Archaic art affects us powerfully just because it is strange and inexplicable. It arises spontaneously, as do the drawings of small children, and its images do not show things as they are seen; moreover, drawings in the Archaic style may have fearful or transcendent effect.

This quality of strangeness and ambiguity can seem intolerable, arousing primitive fear and making us recoil, for art objects alert our own creative impulse to shape and contain the unknown. We look over a painting or sculpture to find the familiar in its strangeness, and if we cannot do this we feel anxious and frustrated. If Archaic art comes from our own hands we are also unable to explain it logically, but its very strangeness imbues it with authority and, however grotesque or repulsive the subject may be, it gives its creator an inexplicable sense of satisfaction.

Figure 7.11 is an example of the ambiguous power of Archaic Linear art. The object is constructed in three dimensions but does not give any impression of weight or volume. If we study it closely we can see that the image has the nightmare quality that fuses subject and object, worshipped and worshipper. It snarls and yet cringes. For this reason it is rather frightening – conjuring up a primitive fear of being eaten or bewitched. This primordial fear is activated as spider phobia, the insect's contaminating unpredictability creating irrational terror, the 'goose-flesh' of a kinaesthetic recoil from the goddess Kali when she wears her necklace of skulls.

THE THERAPEUTIC FUNCTION OF ARCHAIC AND TRADITIONAL ARTS

Traditional art functions to maintain the past in a form that is acceptable to the present. Its images as well as its style may be re-created, as in Ann's *Crinoline Lady*, for instance, but the style maintains the validity of emotional or perceptual/intuitive ways of living to shape represented facts. Thus, the past is visually assimilated into the present and inner reality into the external world.

As I see it, Barbara and Joyce, Jane and Miss Rink were coming to the end of their lives, and when they had made a symbolic image of bereavement it gave them a means of being reconciled to death. Their Traditional art gave access to their feelings and enabled others to share the process of mourning.

Archaic art is a different matter; it has little conscious content and may be completely unintelligible both to the viewer and to its creator, for it presents a visible image of the unconscious primeval psychic life of the senses that Freud discovered through interpreting dreams and described as a 'primordial language' that is permanently unconscious and 'not merely latent at the moment' (Freud 1961: 16, 140).

Because sensuous experience has little place in conscious life, we respond to its imagery with surprise or incredulity. We feel that the shapes which suddenly appear, without our thinking about them, are mad or childish. If we cannot dismiss them they make us uneasy, even frightened or horrified if they appear in association with thoughts of death, for the sensuous reaction to bereavement is fear, mindless fear of the unknown. Our ghost stories reflect this fear in tales of invisible bodies hidden beneath a sheet or skeletons that shift unpredictably, like the sudden jump of a spider.

The Archaic Linear style, being the earliest form of art, carries within it the most primitive attempts at symbol formation:

> Symbol formation is an activity of the ego attempting to deal with the anxieties stirred by its relation to the object and is generated primarily by fear of bad objects and the fear of the loss or inaccessibility of good objects . . . disturbances in relation between the ego and object lead to disturbances in differentiation between the symbol and the object symbolized and therefore to the concrete thinking characteristic of psychosis.
>
> (Segal 1986: 52)

For years I responded to the aesthetic beauty and simplicity of Archaic Linear art (Figure 1.11) while also recognizing the hypnotic effect that could hold an artist to the present, like Rip Van Winkle, absorbing him in creative bondage to the sensuous reality of iconic images. Now I can see how this narrow vision can enable some people to come to the end of life with equanimity. My final example of bereavement art shows how it can occur.

DR WILL

Although the people described in this chapter suffered the stress of physical handicaps they were not mentally ill but retained normal defences in the conditions of life in geriatric hospital or residential home. However, these patients needed opportunities to image their past and their future, to look back on their lives and forward to death.

Dr Will was seventy, suffering from increasing disabilities caused by Parkinson's disease that he bore with patience and humour. Although he never volunteered to join an art group, he was too courteous to refuse when any of its members invited him to share a painting session with them. He made coloured drawings with paint or pastel in an Archaic Linear style and seemed to find the results surprising, inviting humorous interpretation.

On the occasion of his final painting he chose yellow paper, placed horizontally; on this he drew a circle in white paint enclosing another, bisected by a row of white dots and dashes. Then he added lines with brownish purple paint, extending these symmetrically as two rectangles that contained lines and smears, suggesting eyes. The whole design was elaborated on the left by a line that continued in arrow form, while the right was shaped like a bow, or bracket (Figure 7.12).

The whole design was framed with a strong blue line on three sides, the left hand edge being open and the bottom line completed by a scribbled flourish, like a signature added when a picture is completed.

Dr Will seemed as surprised as usual by this drawing but this time he did not treat it as a joke but studied it thoroughly. Later he took a separate

Figure 7.12 Metamorphic design

piece of paper and made a note about it which he did not show to anyone; it was found later, placed under the drawing.

Archaic Linear art is often abstract: without subject matter a picture is wide open to imaginative projections and this painting was no exception. Although it was a spontaneous doodle, the way it was painted, the lines and colours strongly suggested meaning but his note only described the way it had occurred. My own impression was of a frightened face, mutely screaming.

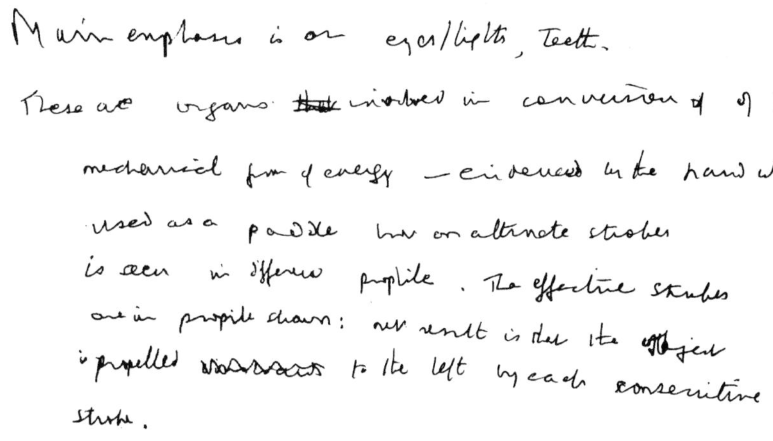

Main emphasis is on eyes/lights, Teeth.

These are organs involved in conversion of ? into

mechanical form of energy — evidenced by the hand which is

used as a paddle how on alternate strokes

is seen in different profile. The effective strokes

are in profile drawn: nett result is that the object

is propelled ~~~~ to the left by each consecutive

stroke.

Figure 7.13 A facsimile of Dr Will's note

Dr Will's note illustrates the great difficulty anyone finds when trying to discuss Archaic Linear art, for the style symbolizes sensuous reality severed from thought, emotion and appearances of external life.

In my efforts to find adequate words to describe the symbolism of Archaic art I turned to psychoanalytic theories: Freud's concept of primary thought as *visual* reminded me that the Archaic Linear style occurs spontaneously in children's first drawings. As images of primary mental processes, they are shaped by a 'body ego' that has little or nothing to do with the complexities of conceptual thought.

I found in Michael Balint the discovery that preconditions for creative activity could be inferred from a particular mental state or area in which there is no external object. This means that a patient or artist is totally *on his own* and 'his main purpose is to create something out of himself' (Balint 1979: 24). For example, it is remarkable that a little child knows, somehow from himself, how to draw in his own style.

Balint's observation of the imperviousness of primary creativity seemed to link with my experience of an autistic boy who showed quite exceptional fearlessness in balancing on the narrow ledges of rocks, but was extremely frightened by the distant approach of a dog. This seemed to me to reflect a split between abnormal consciousness of the sensuous reality of his body and anxieties about possible hazards in the external world.

Marion Milner drew attention to the external component of body ego, describing changes in the physical appearance of a patient

> who would at times have moments of startling physical beauty counter-balanced by moments of something startlingly repellent. One could certainly think of this phenomenon in terms of complete union with a marvellous or atrocious object, with the obliteration of inner boundaries between the ego and the incorporated object.
>
> (Milner 1987: 95)

This observation seemed to fit my idea of the effect of sensuous dominance that provides the ballet-like coordination necessary to make the perfect circles and straight lines of Archaic Linear art. Her idea of a patient being possessed by the incorporated object is a subtler way of describing the creative impulse that is more usually described as inspiration. Moreover, the idea of the artist being 'taken over' by an inner object fits my observation that Archaic Linear images can be replicated in an almost hallucinatory way.

Dr Will died less than 24 hours after making his picture and when I first read his note I was puzzled by its emotional detachment. It was difficult to believe that he had created the image that I saw, or that its creation had been in any sense therapeutic. I had come to see the Circle having paramount importance in the face of death, marking the boundary between Self and Other. In some paintings made at the end of his life the Circle was associated with immortality: Joyce's fountain, Barbara's eye of wisdom and Miss Rink's primeval sun all used the symbol in a context that substantiated this meaning in the subject matter. Dr Will's art lacked apparent content: all I had was his note, and my 'gut reaction' to inform me.

I found a reason for the difference between Dr Will's stated view of his painting and my own through Freud's hypothesis of two complementary instincts. Although he recognized that fusion of opposites was characteristic of primary mental processes, logical description demanded of him the concept of instinct split into opposite tendencies:

> the erotic instincts, which are always trying to collect living substances together into ever larger unities, and the death instincts which act against that tendency and try to bring living matter back into an inorganic condition. The cooperation and opposition of these two forces produce the phenomena of life to which death puts an end.
>
> (Freud 1961: 152)

In Dr Will's last picture a methodical arrangement of incomplete squares symbolize the immanent dissolution of his external life. I, and some others like myself who are governed by the instinct to stay alive, could only see this as the tragic background to a Circle of inaudible terror, but the fact remained, Dr Will had not reacted in this way to his painting, but with curiosity and satisfaction. His painting must have provided him with a positive symbol of integration. Turning again to Freud, I came to understand how this could be.

> The hypothesis of self-preservative instincts, such as we attribute to all living beings, stands in marked opposition to the idea that instinctual life as a whole serves to bring about death. Seen in this light, the theoretical importance of the instincts of self-preservation, of self-assertion and of mastery greatly diminishes. They are component instincts whose function it is to assure that the organism shall follow its own path to death, and to ward off any possible ways of returning to inorganic existence other than those which are immanent in the organism itself. ... What we are left with is the fact that the organism wishes to die only in its own fashion.
>
> (Freud 1950: 513)

By writing his note, Dr Will extended his art to bridge the inarticulate life of sensuous reality towards conscious comprehension, and affirmed the *process* as the therapeutic function of the style.

FOREKNOWLEDGE IN PSYCHO-PHYSICAL LIFE

Thinking in images precedes verbal thought:

> our thoughts originated in such perceptual forms; their earliest material and the first stages in their development consisted in sense impressions or, more accurately, of memory-pictures of these. It was later that words were attached to these pictures and then connected so as to form thoughts
>
> (Freud 1961: 152)

Consequently, translation of visual into verbal thought confines the symbol into a concept of the inherent meaning. A spontaneously created image, being symbolic, inevitably transcends this limitation to logical thought and makes available to consciousness the psychosomatic awareness of the Self as a whole. Although sensuous life is, to a great extent, unconscious, it is projected upon anything that is neutral enough to receive it. Abstract patterns or meaningless scribbles may be used in this way to create images of the primary mental processes that can then become organized in secondary elaborations of thought. These symbolic images of primary processes appear as simple geometric shapes, symbolizing the Self as a Circle. Squares symbolize all that is not perceived as the Self.

As I continued to study Dr Will's last painting I began to understand how the creative process had allowed him to realize and work through the primitive anxieties that had seemed so insoluble when I first saw the completed work. I began to follow the brownish-purple lines as developments within his psyche and this enabled me to withdraw my projection of them as alien forces that had caused his death.

The line that seems to reach out to the left and then double back upon itself and point inward with a distinct arrow-shaped head now could be seen as the realization that the destructive force came from within himself; the right-hand shape was the bow.

Although the lines were only used as an abstract design, Dr Will had chosen where they should go. It seemed to me that he had unconsciously confirmed the sensuous reality while maintaining the basic integrity of the white Circle of his essential Self, much as Miss Rink had painted the forces of destruction in her own way and also affirmed the certainty of an enduring sense of Self in the Archaic Circle of the sun.

SYMBOLIC CONTENT IN BEREAVEMENT ART

All creative art is symbolic, that is, it implies far more than it represents in its subject-matter, and its images reach beyond our powers of description.

The opportunity to realize symbolic meaning in a work of art is dependent upon a mood that allows for varying ways of looking at things, and an ability to respond differently to the same object or person and to accept that we can feel differently towards the same thing. Once a thought or emotion is fully determined it is no longer used as a symbol. What we interpret we inevitably transfer into an idea, but the symbol itself remains enigmatic, challenging our imagination further. A work of art retains this potency, and any attempt to interpret symbolic images totally can only end in 'and – and – and'.

This is the essence of art as therapy and the therapist must beware of defining visual symbols as fixed signs.

> The creative activity of the imagination frees man from his bondage to the 'nothing but' and liberates him in the spirit of play.
>
> (Jung 1947: 76)

Thus Jung speaks of the power of art to activate us; yet I also need a commonly accepted standpoint to describe its effect, otherwise I must remain isolated in subjective judgement, dependent upon a projection of my own creative imagination; then I cannot be sure how much I have taken from the artist and how much I have imposed upon his work. Consequently, when I describe paintings by Ann and Joyce, Barbara, Jane, Miss Rink and Dr Will, I must abstract myself from the intimacy permitted to those who share unspoken assumptions and separate out any recurring element expressing a resolution of bereavement that would account for the satisfaction and comfort they achieved through painting.

ANN

Although Ann rejected her clay model, the little figure presented symbols of the span of life visualized with a clarity of perceptive intuition. This view of reality includes an emotional reserve and intuitive understanding. But Ann was not able or ready to use her habitual attitude, and her defence against bereavement suffering blocked her creative initiative. Moreover, the external conditions of the art class did not provide the privacy she needed and Traditional Massive art was too close to external reality to be concealed within the artifice of a sentimental figurine. Her conscious intention was blocked by her unconscious need to attend to her bereavement.

Death of a spouse leaves the bereaved partner with the loss of creative potential through sexual life and when Ann effaced this effect in her model she was left with an alternative that seemed intolerable – the inevitability of old age. While Ann was in this mood of denial she could only see her work negatively, as Jung puts it, as 'nothing but'.

JOYCE

Joyce also had great difficulty in letting go her desire to plan and control her life. She fought disease from this position and, like Ann, her determination to maintain conscious control pinned her art to an inflexible form of the Traditional Linear style in which everything must have clear boundaries, contrasts and demarcation lines. In these harsh restrictions was no room at all for 'the spirit of play'. If we look at the first example of her work (Figure 7.2) it shows how she clung to the basic symbol of outer reality as a Square, shaped as a rustic arch. The harshness of this artificial shape was imposed upon the idea of natural beauty that it was intended to express. Then the dream of the fountain provided a beautiful motif for the Circle of Self and allowed her emotion to shape the image as a Massive transitional form in which inner and outer reality merge in harmony. Absorbed in her painting, Joyce was able to appreciate the supernatural implication of the magnificent fountain where the waters of life flowed from, and into, eternal seas.

BARBARA

Barbara's response to clay was direct. She immediately sensed the symbolic potential of the plastic medium by pressing it into flat slabs that she interpreted as a metaphor for her boxed-in life. As she did not associate the oblong shape with a coffin, I saw that she was not ready to face this eventuality and my intervention supported this by asking what she might put inside the box. Her angry negative response, arising within her creative impulse, enabled her to discover the eye of wisdom within her crushing hand. In terms of basic symbolism, Barbara moved from the Square to the Circle containing the wisdom of an inner eye.

JANE

This patient alerted me to the positive aspect of Traditional Linear art when it is used flexibly to express inner and outer reality. Her initial use of the style was fragmented and the ideas it contained were disconnected, limited to pictorial signs, but quite soon she organized them into coherent memories and established an attitude of warm and humorous regard for her past and present life. In her last two paintings, of the cottages for sale, she reached beyond this style to include some perceptual recollections by introducing paint that she tinted to a shade she remembered.

The basic symbols could be discerned in the small, unobtrusive Circle of the clock faces she introduced in her first drawings and the sun drawn as a Linear shape in the picture *Cottages for Sale* (Figure 7.9).

Jane came to the end of her life with equanimity. She had created art in 'the spirit of play', released from the depressing sense of 'nothing but'.

MISS RINK

Others in the old people's home where she lived for the last years of her life looked to this old lady for the moral strength and reasonableness that is often needed in establishments of this kind. Both staff and patients depended on her and mourned her loss. Her art reflected a rational, perceptive attitude in the Traditional Massive style and she developed the content of a single seascape to balance symbolic images of life and death as light-ship and destroyer, lighthouse and wreck. Finally, when it seemed that she had equalized positive and negative images, death was not to be denied and Miss Rink challenged its hidden purpose in the symbolic image of a speeding torpedo, then responded to this unconscious message of destruction by overpainting her naturalistic image of the sun with the symbolic Circle as a rayed orb, symbolizing regeneration.

DR WILL

Working with people who may be at the end of their lives has special poignancy and stress. I cannot be sure that any symbolic image in the Archaic Linear, abstract style is an unconscious projection or only

Plate 1 Child painting with yellow

Plate 2 Child painting a green circle

Plate 3 Child overpainting the circle

Plate 4 Saint Climent de Taüll (Archaic Linear). Photo: MNAC Photographic Service (Calveras/Sagristà). By permission of the Museu d'Art de Catalunya. Barcelona

Plate 5 Gorse on a Sea Wall by Graham Sutherland (Archaic Massive). By permission of DACS

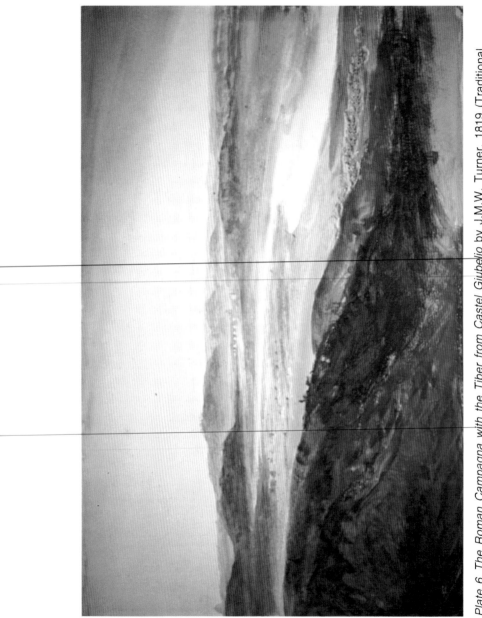

Plate 6 The Roman Campagna with the Tiber from Castel Giubelio by J.M.W. Turner, 1819 (Traditional Massive). By permission of the British Museum

Plate 7 Mr and Mrs Stanley Joscelyne/The Second Marriage by Anthony Green R.A., 1972 (Traditional Linear). By permission of the Anthony Green R.A. Collection, Ulster Museum, Belfast

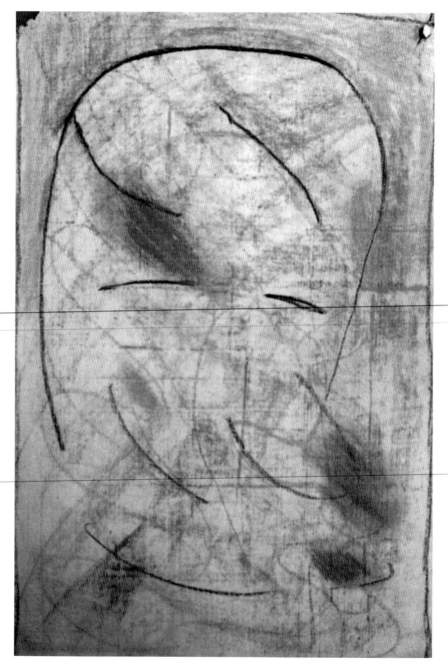

Plate 8 Archaic transition

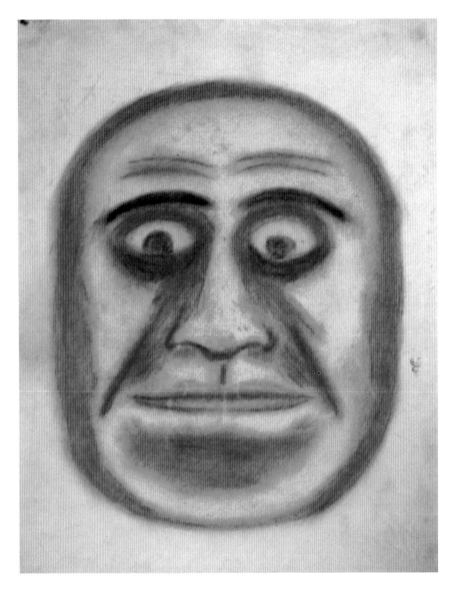

Plate 9 Archaic Massive

Plate 10 Peter's early landscape, Archaic Massive

Plate 11 Peter's later landscape, Traditional Massive

Plate 12 The Church Garden, Massive transition

Plate 13 *Rain on the Pavement*, Archaic Massive

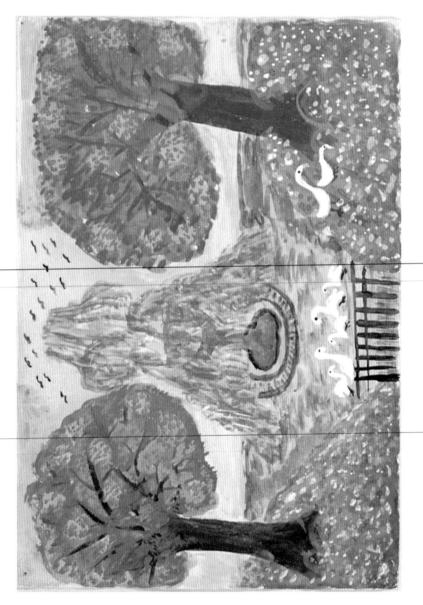

Plate 14 Fountain in the Sea, Massive transition

Plate 15 *The Happy Hunting Ground*, Massive transition

Plate 16 Viking Ship

recognized through counter-transference. Dr Will's last drawing had the immediacy of a shock for me but it did not appear to affect him in this way. This might have been a case of projective identification (Segal 1986), his unconscious terror being projected into me. I came to understand the difference in our reactions when I recalled the *process* of its creation as distinct from the created *product*. This could be likened to a sequence of words that make up the meaning of a sentence. I recalled the process of its creation by the order in which the lines had been made, in this way I could follow its making, from the first mild assertions – Dr Will's choice of a pale yellow paper and the central, white circle painted in the centre of it.

I could then go on to identify the Circle as the symbol of the Self, that had originally appeared to be a screaming orifice. Then I followed the second white, enclosing Circle with its straight base line and the darker overpainting emphasizing three-quarters of it on the right-hand side and extending up and along to form an incomplete purplish line curved out from the circle and returning in an irregular line, arrow-headed back into the square. How was it that these painted gestures helped, supported or resolved an unconscious foreknowledge of death when so many of the shapes had been left incomplete?

It appears that those who spontaneously create images of bereavement use a style that reflects a means of resolution, whether this be conceptual or emotional, intuitive or the kind of sensuous reality that shaped the painting of Dr Will. I can only imagine that death itself provides the ultimate experience of resolution, and that the living cannot know the sense of completion that held William Blake when he painted and sang ecstatically on his deathbed.

FOUR FACES OF REALITY

According to our changing moods we see things differently: one day we can laugh at things that depress or infuriate us at another time. The style of a work of art reflects the artist's mood at the time. This mood may have been provoked by the subject-matter or held consistently as a habitual attitude. The image may be rational or sensuous, fill us with gentle nostalgia or strong emotion, each individual unthinkingly shaping his art to picture his view of reality.

Bereavement art, the focus of this chapter, presents these different ways of seeing the reality of death: our need to integrate the external reality of finite life with the inner sense of an abiding self that is an inextricable part of human consciousness.

Archaic arts reveal the sensuous and emotional attributes we ascribe to Self and Others. These ignore the external realities of space and time; they cannot envisage death as an individual end in continuing life.

Traditional styles can contain the perceived reality of physical death and the ideas that we construct about personal mortality.

Ann's effortless perception of external reality gave her immediate access to creative initiative, but it became intolerable when it reflected the suppressed reality of her loss.

Joyce could not think about death until she had found a symbolic image that combined a perception of its reality with an evaluation of it as a strange, but beautiful condition.

Barbara's box was planned and assembled piece by piece, first seen as a simple metaphor for her frustrating life. Then she discovered 'the third eye' and with it an intuitive perception of objects she could hardly see.

Jane was one whose positive use of thinking restored her humorous attachment to life and Miss Rink responded to an abstract doodle by creating images of preservation and destruction against each other. When she was coming close to death her 'laid-back' attitude did not suffice and she imposed a symbolic image of inner reality upon a rational view of the external world.

Dr Will seemed to live in the eternal present of sensuous reality.

THE THERAPEUTIC FUNCTION OF THE STYLES IN BEREAVEMENT ART

My understanding of therapy in creative art is concerned with the symbolic power of imagery to reach beyond the boundaries of verbal thought. This occurs not when art is taken literally, but when it acts as a symbolic image through our understanding of content and its style. This is its essential value as therapy, that which Jung speaks of as the power to 'activate' us.

> The creative activity of the imagination frees man from his bondage to the 'nothing but' and liberates him in the spirit of play.
>
> (Jung 1947: 76)

In bereavement art the patient's unconscious drive to substitute symbolic realization for the bald fact of death or blind denial of it released symbolic imagery for Barbara, Joyce, Jane and Miss Rink. Creative art challenges our imagination to reach beyond the known, but it always needs a safe place where it can be seen and heard.

I will draw out the particular function of the styles used by these patients in order to focus on their particular values as psychic containers for bereavement.

The Traditional Massive style is recognized by its naturalistic proportions; these re-create the external conditions of coexistence.

The Traditional Linear style of Joyce's *Paradise Garden* (Figure 7.2) was unable to contain the emotional conflict that she, like Ann, could not face; but Joyce had the concerned attention of her doctors, and her dreams allowed her to value their style as realistic visions of her life to come.

Barbara's Massive style enabled her to relax the limitations of Traditional Linear art. Her mood shifted as she responded to the head with its third eye (Figure 7.3). This work seemed to take away her frustration about the painful limitation of her life. In the Traditional Massive naturalism of *The Skull* and *The Foot* (not illustrated) the moderate attitude that they reflect showed that they were created without distress, as perceptive recollections. I think both *The Skull* and *The Third Eye* sculptures bore some resemblance to her dead father, and this may well have sustained her intuitive perception of approaching death.

Jane's Traditional Linear painting revealed the positive value of a logical and factual attitude that does not rigidly confine emotions or religious convictions. While painting, Jane sometimes sang hymns and her subject-matter showed an affectionate and humorous attitude usually found in Archaic Massive art; however, her use of writing drew work such as Figures 7.9 and 7.10 towards the style I designate as a Linear transition. Her last picture also came to suggest a poetic quality of religious experience when she added the huge, 'embracing' shape of a building behind the row of cottages. If I am right in seeing this as 'my Father's House in which there are many mansions', it would reflect her religious belief and the generosity of her habitual attitude.

Miss Rink's Traditional Massive style is consistent with her intuitive perceptions of objective reality, recollected in light and space. This attitude allowed her to make a naturalistic painting without effort but, before this work was quite finished, she needed to include the symbolism of eternal life in the detail of the Archaic sun. This essential need to realize the sense of Self shocked and enraged the priests in Blake's poem when *A Little Boy Lost* announced:

> Nought loves another as itself.
> Nor venerates another so,
> Nor is it possible to thought
> A greater than itself to know.

> (Blake 1939: 385)

This assertion is the spring of creativity that unconsciously lifts dying or bereaved adults and children above the crushing effects of their suffering. But the creative impulse requires an appropriate space and time to form its object, and this is sometimes lacking. Ann and Joyce, for example, found great difficulty in reaching beyond their habitual defences against inner reality; for Ann, the place was not safe enough and for Joyce time was needed for her defences to be withdrawn – time, and that wonderful dream. For such people, the therapeutic integration may not be achieved in one image; more time is needed for more paintings. This may be especially true of Archaic Linear art, which is highly potent but without perceptual or conceptual elements that would allow a message to be understood.

The Archaic Linear style reflects the sensuous reality of the body that is our instinctual life. Normally, this is extended in consciousness by emotions or ideas, and shock is the direct response of unmodified instinctual life. Death is then the loss of the symbolic modifications that are constructed in the mind as a modifying defence against shock. Archaic art is a symbolic realization of sensuous life, stripped, as it were, of emotional colouring, intuitive relating and our powers of thought. Archaic Linear art is itself, stark, omnipotent and uncompromising.

In my previous book (Simon 1991) I described difficulties I have found in this art form as a therapy. Therapy implies change in an unconscious attitude, but the artist who habitually uses this style is dominated by the sensuous life and this, together with the artist's defences against it, may form a deadlock, so that the art is fixed and stereotyped.

TRADITIONAL LINEAR ART AS POETRY

Although the effort to abstract verbal thought from its symbolic image may rob it of its visual associations, the art of writing extends its imagery through allegory and poetry, allowing symbolic associations to accrue to function as therapy. I will confine myself to a very few instances of symbolic imagery in poems that indicate something of the way their aesthetic structure indicates their function in expressing feelings and thoughts through the style of their presentation.

Some adults and older children may have times when they are unable to work with paint or clay in any depth. Children may flit from work to work, covering paper with a few marks or graffiti, slogans or cartoon images that, although they emerge from the patient's impulse for self-expression, say little more than that there is a wish to invade or destroy an empty, or a potential space. Some react like Ann, by giving up and going away. Some adults get stuck in a style, and it binds them to a way of thinking, or similarly they may endlessly repeat a stereotyped landscape or face. At some point, if they do not give up or have, like Joyce, an inspiring dream, I may feel that I cannot bear this stasis. I may not know whether it is my identification with the patient's desperate need to act or if it is my own frustration. Often the simplest aids are the most successful – providing an extra lamp, an easel rather than the flat table, new colours or a nice boxwood modelling tool – little is needed to demonstrate concern for the creative process. A notebook and pencil amongst the art equipment may invite a story or a poem.

Some adults turn naturally to poetry if their pictorial art has become fixed in the factualism of Traditional Linear art and its stereotypes, but any visual association can release a poem. Many adolescents whose visual art has been blocked can be helped by images that 'speak' for them in poems or prose.

The poem that heads this chapter presents the idea of death as a truth that 'does not lie', and now I will add to it another poem that was written by the same young man at an earlier time.

Not all die so hard or so young and lonely as this man whose despair deeply concerned his doctors and nurses. He was terminally ill, living in a single hospital room, deeply depressed and appeared to be without family or friends. He had refused art materials but I continued to visit him in hope that something more helpful might occur.

At last, one day he gave me a poem and although I did not understand it I was very relieved to find that he had created something. I wish that I could have tuned in to the positive symbolism that now, many years after, seems so clear to me.

NEVER TO KNOW

Never to know the hand
behind the touch,
sight, sound, name,
of table, chair –
The name of the lover.
Is this death?
This final ignorance?
Never to know the substance
from the shadow's
web over life's living form?

Is death the death of a web
cast on reality?

The dying patient expresses the pain of bereavement as the lack of meaning. Like Jane's early painting, the poem's style seems to fragment his thought. Its images shift between the outer world of tables and chairs and the loss of a lover he does not know. The poem's symbolic imagery is of alienation, but the style is a structured and aesthetically satisfying form.

When I first read this poem I was concerned with the theme of a lost lover and overlooked the expression of his alienation.

Balint (1986) emphasizes the importance of giving expression to the mood that he describes as the area of creativity. This man had the creative power to hold a negative, helpless state of mind and to express it in the positive ordering structure of words. The pain and fear of death is contained by the poetic voice that images a universal fear of being trapped in a web where he would be bereft of love as well as life, the everyday life of tables and chairs. This young man's poem offered no comfort, only a question.

I found the poem painful although I was relieved that he had broken out of his inertia; the brutal truth enabled him to communicate bitterness and his poem made me share his experience. There was no flash of relief or enlightenment. I was left with the dead weight of his despair, but he was lightened because he had given form to a nameless dread and this I understood later when he wrote other poems.

The power of creativity is greater than we observe it from the outside. It is only when we have written a poem or painted a picture, however insignificant to anyone else, that we experience the power released by creative initiative and know for a fact that symbolic images can reach beyond the power of thought.

Psychotherapy has taught us to put our trust in talking, yet it is ineffectual without the poetry that makes talking memorable. The dying man did not speak or listen to us until he wrote the poems.

Jung, writing of art as therapeutic, says:

> We are dealing with a region of psychic life outside consciousness ... it seems to me to be a question of some kind of centring process ... which brings into being a new centre of equilibrium and it is as if the ego turned in an orbit round it. We can only remark on its important effect upon the conscious personality. From the fact that the change heightens the feeling for life and maintains the flow of life we must conclude that a particular purposefulness is inherent in it.
>
> (Jung 1947: 83)

I feel that creative art brought 'into being a new centre of equilibrium' for this man and many other patients whose work I have been privileged to share. The centre of equilibrium seems to be a truth that integrates inner and outer reality. Here I repeat the poem I used to preface this chapter:

NO MORE LYING
You and I must surely die.
Death does not cheat or lie
So why should I?

SUMMARY

Bereavement means to be bereft, robbed, deprived and left desolate, alone, forlorn and disconsolate. This chapter describes how creative arts are a means of working through the sense of bereavement in terminally ill patients who paint and use poetry.

REFERENCES

Ackroyd, P. (1995) *Blake*, London: Sinclair-Stevenson.
Balint, M. (1986) *The Basic Fault*, London: Tavistock.
Blake, W. (1939) *Poems and Prophesies*, London: J. M. Dent & Sons Ltd.
Freud, S. (1949) *New Introductory Lectures on Psycho-Analysis*, London: Hogarth Press.
—— (1950) *Beyond the Pleasure Principle*, London: Hogarth Press.
—— (1961) *Introductory Lectures on Psycho-analysis*, London: Allen & Unwin.
Jung, C. G. (1947) *Modern Man in Search of a Soul*, London: Kegan Paul
Milner, M. (1986) *On Not Being Able to Paint*, London: Heinemann.
—— (1987) *The Suppressed Madness of Sane Men*, London and New York: Tavistock.
Segal, H. (1986) *The Work of Hanna Segal*, New York: Free Association Books.
Simon, R. M. (1991) *The Symbolism of Style*, London: Routledge.
Winnicott, D. W. (1971) *Playing and Reality*, London: Tavistock.

Chapter 8

Bereavement art in children

The Angel that presided o'er my birth
Said "Little creature, form'd of Joy & Mirth,
Go love, without the help of any Thing on Earth".

(Blake 1939: 385)

In this chapter I am concerned with different ways in which children meet bereavement suffering and how art as therapy can help them when we can follow their progress through the style and content of their art work.

Bereavement is suffering the loss of the sense of life's continuity. Normally this loss is worked through during alternating moods of remembering and forgetting. This is the process of mourning, but not all bereavement is resolved in this way: there is anger and fear as well as mental pain and in particularly intense states, normal forgetting may become the traumatic reaction of amnesia. Elsewhere I have described such a state in a child who called himself 'The Incredible Hulk' (Simon 1991: 77–8).

Although bereavement is usually worked through in the alternating process of remembering and forgetting, there are some whose suffering seems to reflect a previous bereavement that could not be worked through at the time, that appears to be an unresolved trauma, comparable to a physical shock that caused a temporary paralysis and fragmentation of their immature ego.

Although words may be used to relieve the general sense of loss, in moods that reflect the original trauma there are no words. The loss is experienced sensuously, as a hole or a wound to the body that is beyond grief, before a means of recollecting or the power to symbolize our experience in shapes of meaning had been established. We may glimpse this primary catastrophe in the images given by children who are recovering from states of autism described by Frances Tustin:

Absence was 'goneness' – 'goneness' was a broken thing – 'a black hole' full of a 'nasty prick'. He did not 'think' about these things; he felt he took them into his body . . . anxieties rushed in of uncontrollable physical things. The pain of loss seemed to be experienced as bodily rather than mental pain.

(Tustin 1972: 30

These different ways of experiencing bereavement appear to be reenacted spontaneously in creative art and what I observe as a primary bereavement in children in art therapy may well be a flashback to early states that could not be realized. The creative work of drawing and painting seems to activate an instinctive need to make images of such physiological states, but the older we become the more and deeper are the defences against recollection which block our creative impulses.

Young children have direct access to their sensuous and emotional life and symbolize most of it freely in Archaic forms of art, and older children who use art as therapy may make a therapeutic regression to an Archaic art style to realize these primitive states of psycho-physical pain.

THE THEORY OF PRIMARY BEREAVEMENT

It is always catastrophic for a child to lose a parent, but this catastrophe is doubled if the loss replicates an earlier one.

Winnicott (1971) describes such a primary bereavement as a traumatic loss of continuity of *being* at the earliest stages of life, when the identities of mother and baby are usually merged and, from the baby's point of view, each is the same as the other. In Winnicott's experience the baby is traumatized if, beyond a certain time, he experiences a break in life's continuity.

This concept of a primary bereavement is so fundamental to my understanding of bereavement art that I quote Winnicott at length, interpreting 'the object' as an imaginative creation, even if it is made by a baby's mouth finding its thumb.

> It is perhaps worth while trying to formulate this in a way that gives the time factor its due weight. The feeling of the mother's existence lasts X minutes. If the mother is away more than X minutes the imago fades, and along with this the baby's capacity to use the symbol of the union ceases. The baby is distressed but this distress is soon *mended* because the mother returns in X+Y minutes. In X+Y minutes the baby has not become altered.... But in X+Y+Z minutes the baby has become traumatized. In X+Y+Z minutes the mother's return does not mend the baby's altered state. Trauma implies that the baby has experienced a break in life's continuity.
>
> (Winnicott 1971: 97; emphasis in original)

Although we can do no more than speculate about a baby's experience, it seems that a primary bereavement is traumatic because it lacks the associations that normally provide a means of assimilating a loss through the normal process of mourning. The pain cannot be worked through by the alternating process of forgetting and remembering because the baby has few memory traces that can construct a 'feeling of the mother's existence' and has lost the 'capacity to use the symbol of union' – the symbol that I recognize as a Circle in the Square. The trauma remains unresolved unless it can be displaced upon a later, equivalent experience, when the intensity of the original state can be relived, contained and worked through within the immediate loss.

Therapeutic success for primary and secondary states of bereavement will depend upon the extent to which a child had originally acquired sufficient associations to allow symbols of union and separation to develop in a context. I imagine that this depends upon the innate maturational rate of the individual and the age of the baby or the time – the 'Z' minutes – that had elapsed (Winnicott 1971: 97).

For the therapeutic work to succeed, implicit acceptance of the images is essential and enough time must be allowed for symbolism to prepare the way for conscious or explicit communication. The formation of symbolic images that are meaningless is a particularly sensitive time, for they only communicate to the artist through his eyes and this gestation period should not be aborted by any interpretation. The therapist who is an artist can respond to the visual and non-verbal as more significant than words, for words can obscure meaning as easily as they reveal it. Freedom to use simple art materials allows the child's sensuous and emotional life to be exposed; *then* simple or complex images may come to contribute to the stages of mourning. In this visual way, inarticulate feelings can be projected upon images that can be used to mirror the unconscious feeling as when, for example, apparently extravagant grief is shown by the child who has mislaid a toy or a hair-ribbon, or broken a plate.

This hypothesis is a drastic simplification of the complexity of actual life and I do less than justice to the symbolic imagery of the children I describe as examples of the two sorts of response to bereavement.

First of all, Jennie and Pat were two children who were able to bring or recover many associations with ordinary life to enrich their imaginative world. These enabled them to contain a successful therapeutic regression through art therapy. The girl I call Jennie was retreating from puberty and her art revealed the cause as the loss of parenting she had suffered at the age of seven when she was admitted to a children' home. The boy Pat lived at home, where his family was facing the mother's terminal illness.

The other two children whom I call Sally and Frank had to deal with experiences of primary bereavement and showed the need to make a considerable regression through the creative initiative of their art.

Figure 8.1 The Queen

JENNIE

When I was introduced to this nine-year-old girl who lived in residential care she smiled brightly but did not speak. Her carers had recently become worried about her as she seemed to have withdrawn from the busy life of her group, and her school work had deteriorated. Whenever she could, she slipped away and went to sit on her bed near the many soft toys that were arranged there, against the wall.

At first Jennie did not speak when she came to my studio after school but she worked easily with the paint and clay, showing imagination and dexterity with the materials. Before too long she told stories about the clay models and paintings she made; these were about important people, queens (Figure 8.1), clever girls and adventurous boys.

Her art style was Traditional – detailed paintings in bright local colours of clothes and jewellery. When she began to write poetry it described her defences and reached indirectly, sometimes by omission or in a very roundabout way, towards a sense of loss. I had a sense that her art was an easy, brightly coloured screen that hid something that was not there, as in the following poems about compliance and its golden cover that wrapped up so many things in her poems and hid her unacknowledged bereavement. I have not altered her spelling, grammar or punctuation.

MARY'S PALACE

Once upon a time
Mary had a Palace.
Her beds were covered in Gold
and everywhere that Mary went
People told her to do what she was told.

THE GOOD CHOIR GIRL

The Good choir girl sat on a stool,
She always done the Good Will.
And when the Manager come that day
The girls would laugh at her and play.

She was always happy in the household
And she done everything that she was told.
Her big sister would laugh at her
And all the puddings she would stir.

A work of art interprets itself on many levels and the therapist is drawn to the aspect that seems most relevant at the time. Each art work is a confidential communication and when Jennie gave me these poems she looked at me very carefully, to see that I understood them and that I would not say so.

Whatever else it might contain – remembering that a symbolic image contains a whole cluster of meanings – I thought that Jennie was becoming conscious of her compliance and its threat to her creative initiative. The poem was certainly important to her and she made a richly coloured painting of the choir girl singing in the street (Figure 8.2).

In another poem Jennie began to envisage the bad side of her 'golden' withdrawal:

JOHN'S SPECIAL HAT

John's special Hat
Was rimmed with gold
He always wore that hat
To keep him from the cold.

One day John brought his hat to school
Which really was one against the rule,
All the children laughed and played
Had lots of fun throughout the day,

I asked Jennie if there was more of the poem to come and she said gently, 'Some time'.

Figure 8.2 The Choir Girl

PACING

The therapeutic provision of art, as I understand it, invites patients to pace themselves in their work; should the therapist try to force an issue it will beget counterforce as conscious or unconscious resistance.

The slow surfacing of painful memories through their projection in art work allows time for a child to test out the therapeutic situation and to learn whether it is safe for his or her hidden feelings to escape. The therapist knows that this pacing is governed by resistance to pain and that the art work is an essential part of an unconscious need to grasp experience with conscious understanding.

After months of apparently contented play with paint and clay Jennie was still a puzzle. She continued to be a charming, gentle girl who smiled a lot but whose failures in performance disappointed the staff of the home and her teachers at school, although she was slowly but steadily progressing towards the hopes and fears of impending adolescence.

At last she was able to tell me that she had decided not to aim for grammar-school education even though she had been assumed to be capable of it in earlier years. This was a certainly one reason why she was failing academically, for, although talkative and busy while with me, she was still passive and inattentive at school. There was some concern that she might regress further under the pressures of adolescent life. It was not at all clear to the Social Services that further art therapy would be helpful.

I am now inclined to think that a number of unrecorded circumstances helped her to balance her inner and outer needs during the summer holiday of her eleventh year. It is quite likely that some imperative need to assert herself came at the right time and place, although there seems no doubt that there was a dramatic use of art therapy that occurred in a single painting.

USING THE SELF CIRCLE

One day Jennie had been drawing like a teenager, making a delicate charcoal sketch of a young woman surrounded by the things that she would need – high-heeled shoes, radio and a reclining chair. The adolescent girl herself looked out sweetly from a cloud of softly curling hair. As Jennie prepared to leave the studio I reminded her of the approaching summer holiday break. She gave her customary sweet smile and, taking a brushful of black paint, appeared idly to encircle the face in her drawing, going round and round until a heavy, symmetrical outline transformed the features into those of a young child. To this she added tear-dabbed cheeks, a red dress and a darkened neck that seemed like a lump in the throat.

She then added a title, *A Girl Lost in the Forest*, a sinister-looking bird on the tree and a faint bubble from the child's mouth that said 'Stay here' (Figure 8.3, taken from Simon 1991: 43).

The picture spoke as a form of self-discovery: the style clearly regressing from Traditional to Archaic reflected a change in mood from ideal dreams of a glamorous future to the painful reality of a lost child. We waited together until time had been given to this revelation.

I heard nothing of Jennie until after the summer when, instead of coming for individual sessions, she joined the art group in the children's home with her new friend and they drew hugely and with great satisfaction on the corridor wall. Jennie had shed a chrysalis and was a teenager.

Children who face the loss of a parent have to face a changed world. They feel as if they have been robbed, deprived – a terrible and terrifying thing to happen to anyone, and Jennie's withdrawal into vivid fantasy is not surprising, even though it may have been exceptionally prolonged. Each child's response to death is in accord with his or her basic personality; that is, that bereavement is first met with by an habitual attitude that serves to contain the shock. Some children recover faster than others, and doubtless there are many reasons why this should be, but as I see it Jennie and Pat had not had to meet the loss too soon, before they were able to mourn. This is not at all to minimize their suffering, but it may explain why some children recover more quickly than others.

Figure 8.3 A Girl Lost in the Forest

PAT

Pat, an eight-year-old, reacted violently when his mother was dying in hospital. He acted out his feelings by breaking large, ornamental stones and making holes in the plastered walls of his home. He also ran away and hid for hours.

He was a charming, voluble boy from a secure background but he did not voluntarily speak about his mother or appear to notice the distress he was causing by his behaviour. He remained apparently cheerful and friendly but this defensiveness could not withstand his creative initiative.

Pat often used clay, squeezing and thumping it to make monsters. On one occasion he made a realistic head of a hippopotamus with an open mouth and protruding tongue. I helped him to paint the head as he wanted it to be, black, with the mouth red inside (Figure 8.4).

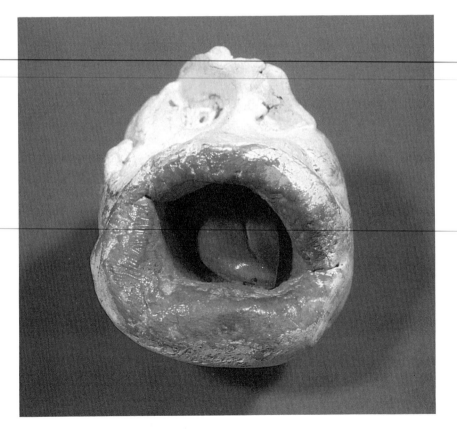

Figure 8.4 The Hippopotamus

THE SHIP BURIAL

I happened to be in another part of the studio one day when I noticed that Pat's mood had changed; he was very quiet, working in a corner, carefully rolling and cutting clay slabs to form a boat, working on this piece for a long time. Having fitted the pieces together to his satisfaction, he separated them again to incise a wave pattern on the sides, the interior and its upper edge. Then he incised a strip of clay with the design of a sun with rays falling onto an ear of corn. This he delicately arranged to hang over the sides. Then he enclosed the prow and decorated this too with a sunburst (Figure 8.5).

The Traditional Linear style of this piece was totally unlike the Massive style he normally used; his thoughtful deliberate work and delicate handling showed willing control of the material. When it was finished he put it on a window-sill to dry.

On another day I offered Pat a small notebook and he immediately sat down at the kitchen table and wrote a poem. When I asked him if he would copy it out for me he seemed pleased to do so. This is the poem:

There is a house far away
With bricks far weaker than clay
And when you sang
Bang, clatter and clang.
But what a horrid place to be,
Even very far from the sea.

Figure 8.5 The Ship Burial

Up in the loft
It is far too soft
And downstairs
It is very bare.
On the roof you can see the sea
And that is where I like to be.

This poem speaks of catastrophe for him. I thought of his cheerfulness
and of the 'bang, clatter and clang' of his destructive behaviour as
distracting chatter that blotted out the pain of his mother's remembered
voice.

Later that day Pat said to me quietly: 'I am sorry for my mother, she
is dying: she has a lot of pain.'

PAT'S USE OF CIRCLES AND SQUARES

Seen as a symbol of Self, Pat's hippopotamus head is a Circle that shows
the gaping wound of his bereavement in the sphere as a tongue in a mouth.
There is little more than two tiny ears to link with the Square of outer
reality. The boat is also a symbol of the self-contained Square of his life,
without oars that could direct his journey into the future. The Square
might be seen in the boat that is collapsed into a triangle. The expression of loss in a symbolic image is a very stabilizing experience, and this
model could be considered as a message of relinquishment, for the boat
will take his mother away. I believe that the image of the boat, so carefully made, reached below his defensive behaviour and allowed him to
speak precisely and accurately in the poem.

Eight-year-old Pat's habitual art style showed an exceptional grasp of
external reality. This was substantiated in the symbolism of his acting out
– he broke stones. (In this he can be compared with Jennie who sat on
her bed.) The hippopotamus is a remarkably naturalistic representation
and the boat was given details that show the full development of his imaginative ideas. Both images are considerable achievements for a young boy.
Pat, as artist and poet, is angry and fearless, able to draw on his perceptual memory and present an image of his loss in the yearning, toothless
mouth and tongue of the hippopotamus without suffering catastrophic
failure of his habitual attitude.

FRANK

As I understand Frank, primary bereavement had badly scarred him,
and his chance of a reasonable life was not clear. He worked with me for
eighteen months, excluding holidays, of weekly, one-hour sessions, from
the time he was taken into care at the age of ten and was causing his

carers anxiety by his fits of panic, violence, soiling and running away or hiding in cupboards.

Eight months earlier, his mother had deserted her five children and, without adult supervision, they had run wild in the countryside, slept rough and played truant from school. Frank and his four-year-old brother were physically neglected and at some stage the little brother died.

Once Frank had been persuaded to sample art therapy he came regularly for weekly sessions, wearing a special cloth cap for the occasion and walking unattended to my studio. He sunned himself in the one-to-one sessions and drew freely in a traditional Massive style (Figure 8.6). Some weeks after his first visit he made a neat pencil drawing of a window in my studio, then slowly and carefully painted out all the details of the white wall with thick black paint (Figure 8.7). This seemed to indicate to me that the blackness of his bereavement could be contained inside the studio, while the view outside the window remained clear. I did not say anything about my impression to this jaunty young boy.

Gradually, Frank's art took on a strongly Archaic style, becoming large, flat and symmetrical (Figure 8.8). He seemed to defend himself sometimes from a sense of chaos by writing football slogans across large pieces of paper – 'just to mess it up or do something'. However, he continued to arrive punctually each week and the staff thought that he enjoyed himself.

Figure 8.6 Keep Out

Figure 8.7 The Window

Figure 8.8 House-face

Figure 8.9 Elives

I think that Frank had experienced primary bereavement as a baby, an experience that was, perhaps, hidden in the needs of his large family. Compared with Pat, whose mother had loved his 'spirit', Frank had to fight for his identity and, in the face of the new group of children in the residential home, had been almost overwhelmed.

Pat could respond to his bereavement with anger and destructiveness but Frank acted his suffering by retreat until he could make a symbolic regression in art. This allowed him to find the emotional strength that appears so clearly in the Archaic *House-face* of Figure 8.8, with the huge black roof like a hat or a burdened mind. This therapeutic regression was most likely to have been the cause of the improvement seen in his behaviour the children's home, where he became continent, happier and less hyperactive.

A clear image of Frank's bereavement denial appeared when a favourite film star died. The death brought forward the children's need to mourn and Frank made a large poster to commemorate the event, but spelling Elvis as 'Elives'. When the mistake was pointed out to him he wrote the name again, but he was still unable to withdraw the symbolism of his spelling (Figure 8.9).

Some children use words or letters as symbolic images, as I have described in my previous book (Simon 1991: 170), but after this incident Frank turned to clay and invented a way of using it stamped or rolled into a flat shape from which he cut a silhouette. This spontaneous use of clay creates Linear images with the sensuous pleasure of ruthless attack on a material, the sweeping assurance of the Archaic Linear artist. This pleasure is obvious in all Archaic art, particularly shown in huge Circles and abstract, geometric shapes, but I think that for Frank it was also a means of controlling his panic by energetically 'working', mastering and inventing a skill that needed thought and preparation. The style reflects the conceptual area of Traditional Linear art and so the work provided a transition between these aptitudes.

Frank mounted some of his silhouettes on off-cuts of wood or card, sometimes painting over the whole thing. He demonstrated this technique by showing me how firmly the wet clay could be stuck down on a panel without glue. On one of these panels a boat was incised with lines and carefully painted black and red, with the oars arranged separately and coloured blue (Figure 8.10). He also modelled some boats in the round, placing them on pedestals made from upturned jam jars; this made them appear like monuments but also marooning them.

Both Frank and Pat could have heard of ship burials in their schools, although neither talked about this way of coming to terms with death. The fact is that both boys produced these images when faced with bereavement. One of Frank's last works was a fine painting on black paper of a

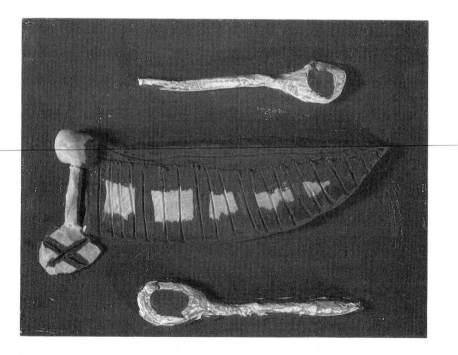

Figure 8.10 Marooned Boat

Viking longship with four occupants and five shields hung over the sides, and an anchor which seemed to be attached to the sky (Plate 16).

Eventually, Frank talked to me about the death of his little brother, giving several conflicting versions until I was able to help him get to the facts at last, with the help of his social worker.

It took Frank and Pat a long time to talk about their suffering. Perhaps Frank did not know about it at first. Both of them had to act out their feelings before they could be offered art as a medium of symbolic communication. When the image had been made, consciousness could follow and the distress could be shared as it edged forward in sad and depressed feelings. When the children could find the words to say what they felt, we could reply and offer practical help.

Here, perhaps, lies the crucial difference between verbal therapy and non-verbal or pre-verbal therapies where patients do not have to talk or remain silent. They actively communicate during times when conscious experience is in abeyance, pre-verbal or mute.

THE WORDLESSNESS OF PRIMARY BEREAVEMENT

Freud helps us to understand this primary level of experience:

> The ego is first and foremost a body-ego; it is not merely a surface entity, but is itself the projection of a surface, i.e., the ego is ultimately derived from bodily sensations, chiefly from those springing from the surface of the body. It may be thus regarded as a mental projection of the surface of the body.
>
> (Freud 1949: 3)

From this I understand that primary bereavement is the loss of someone who, by their ongoing physical contact of touch, smell and sound, if not sight, symbolized the boundary of the infantile self, the body-ego that does not distinguish between the surface that touches and the surface touched. This paradoxical state of sameness in difference is visible in the symbolic image of a Circle in Square, where the area of the Circle is also the inner limit of the area of the Square (Figure 1.1).

Enid Balint helps me to find words for these wordless states and has given an acutely sensitive description of the sort of therapeutic receptivity that is needed to recognize the image of fragmentation that may be used by adults, and by children.

> she began to draw. Her drawing was made up of little lines and dots and, although disconnected, gradually they filled up the whole sheet of paper. She then took another sheet of paper and did the same thing again. This activity was not undertaken easily, as if giving pleasure or

satisfaction, but with intensity and great effort. It was not important that I did not then or later understand and interpret her drawings; but I had always to recognize them as communications, respect them and respond to them.

(Balint 1993: 44)

FRANK'S ARCHAIC ART

Archaic art forms are innate, pre-verbal images of emotional and sensuous reality, symbolized as abstract geometric shapes that are with or without formal attributes. Such images first appear in art's prehistory, to recur in the first drawings of little children and provide a language for regression when art is used as therapy (Simon 1991).

Frank did not return to the Traditional style while he was in therapy until the last sessions, when he had decided that he no longer had time to continue. Then he modelled a book and painted it blue, with yellow edges to the pages. Week after week this book was cut down in size and finally covered perfectly with plastic film. The book was placed on the window-ledge and I took its message to say that his story could, or should, be closed and sealed.

SALLY

As a child, Sally had responded violently to a primary bereavement. When discord between her mother and herself revived the trauma it became intolerable and she ran away and took some dangerous drugs. Her mother deeply regretted mishandling Sally at that time and did what she could to mend things later on. She talked to me very freely about this failure to give her daughter the love she needed and asked me to help. Sally's feelings became intolerable when her mother was forced to withdraw finally into terminal illness and death.

Sally worked in my studio for an hour a week. At first her output was chaotic, hasty and inconclusive; she used clay, making quantities of small objects and figures that were scattered all over the worktop. In spite of her hasty execution, however, the little models were deftly constructed and clearly recognizable. When she felt more at home she began to slow down and drew my attention to one image or another and, as I became drawn in, I was invited to listen to what they had to say, and reply to them. Although the models were made in a very few minutes, they gave rise to long speeches; each image had a voice – the mother, the daughter, the baby and the watch, all explaining how they felt. She began to group them and I wrote down and read back to her all that they said. She seemed to need the structure of my intervention;

Figure 8.11 Mother and Baby

my writing and reading back required her to stay with the images and she came to be interested, then pleased and rather proud of her creative work.

THERAPY AS PLAY

Although art therapy is an intensely serious matter of sanity and madness, it functions as a form of play that can be shared:

> Psychotherapy takes place in the overlap of two areas of playing, that of the patient and the therapist. Psychotherapy has to do with two people playing together.
>
> (Winnicott 1971: 38)

One day Sally modelled a mother holding a baby in her arms, with another little child standing before her. The mother gazes at the little child who stands with her hands behind her back, staring at the mother figure with a tragic expression (Figures 8.11, 8.12 and 8.13).

Sally slowly worked towards realization of the primary bereavement through her exceptionally perceptive understanding. The mother and daughter look sadly at each but do not converse together in the poem; Sally used the little child to talk about them to me in tones of quiet reserve.

Figure 8.12 Detail of *Mother and Baby*

While Sally's art remained traditional it showed her sympathy with the mother, the baby and even herself in the image of the little daughter; but she was still unaware of the self-destructive passion that she had once enacted in a suicide gesture. I do not mean that her art was a conscious or intellectual effort to understand her mother, but that the intuitive insights forming the Traditional Massive style inevitably modify the intensity of emotional experience. If Sally had told me that her mother had been busy and worried by the new baby I might have thought that she was repeating hearsay, perhaps as a way of excusing her own jealousy. However, the Traditional Massive style offered a

Figure 8.13 Child with Hands behind Back

Figure 8.14 Mother (with Large Watch) and Baby

Figure 8.15 Child with Starry Eyes

Figure 8.16 Medusa Mask

positive statement, showing Sally's intuitive response to her mother's predicament. Intuition may not be altogether conscious but it is the faculty that is usually dominant during the second half of childhood. While working with this sensitive girl I was constantly reminded of Chris, the young man whose intuitive understanding of his girlfriend had prevented him from working through his anger towards her. His destructiveness had been turned against himself in agoraphobia (Simon 1991: 21–30).

Some time later Sally made the mother and child again. They reflected her need to regress to an Archaic art and meet the destructive feelings that belonged to the primary bereavement. In this version of mother, child and baby the figures are larger and more active. The mother figure seems to sway, her arms wrap round her baby like a clamp and she wears a huge watch strapped to her wrist (Figure 8.14). The little child seems older now, perhaps about seven, and she seems to be shouting, staring at her mother with 'starry' eyes, reaching out to her a bowl and spoon. Her expression is difficult to understand – is she crying or shouting? Her eyes might be marked by teardrops or sparkling with a challenging anger (Figure 8.15).

HATE AND FEAR IN BEREAVEMENT ART

Sally's art at this time had seemed associated with feelings of guilt and sympathy that are in normal mourning, but when her art regressed to the Archaic Massive style it released her fear and rage; she could not mourn for the loss of a loved and loving mother until she had worked through the primal bereavement that she was known to have suffered when she was about two years old and her sister was born.

Through the illusion of art Sally was able to suspend her defence of intuitive understanding. As she worked the clay the mother image that came to her was a mask of Medusa (Figure 8.16), the snake-haired Gorgon who turned hearts to stone. Sally's mother had been able to help her a great deal in the later part of her childhood, as I could see both from the development of her intuitive attitude and from the Traditional Massive image of the Medusa that was, after all, presented as a mask.

Sally's intuitive attitude accommodated her early experiences with passive acceptance that had become an illness, expressed by running away and a suicide attempt; but something of her mother's concern had got through to Sally, as I saw from the Medusa head that was only a mask. Nevertheless, Sally as a baby had suffered a traumatic break in her sense of continuity and the intuitiveness had been, in part, a defence against

> a repetition of unthinkable anxiety or a return to the acute confusional state that belongs to the disintegration of nascent ego structure.
>
> (Winnicott 1971: 97)

THERAPEUTIC REGRESSION

When primary bereavement is uncovered, the work of art is an essential means of containment. Sally's art was a vital link between her unconscious trauma and her mother's death.

When her art style changed from small, rather naturalistic images to the crude, bodiless mask of the Archaic myth, her response to bereavement changed and her habitual attitude of perceptive reasoning gave way to agonizing rage. But this time she did not run away or make a suicidal gesture; instead she shaped her feelings in dwarf-like images and bitter, sarcastic poetry. In spite of the violence of these feelings Sally did not destroy the earlier figures or feel forced to deny their pity; making the Medusa head allowed her to view her conflicting feelings side by side rather than as a series of disembodied thoughts.

MOURNING

Once Sally's original trauma had been fully shaped by her creative art, mourning could begin its natural oscillation between remembering and forgetting that had been confused by the coincidence of her two bereavements. The image of the older child allowed Sally to express her feelings about the mother figure's remoteness and her own need to distance herself from the past.

THE 'CHILD'S' POEM

. . .

The table is standing straight and erect,
as if knowing what is around him
But I'm sure he knows more
About this family
Than we do, ourselves.

He knows every move, and action
That his family is going to make
Yet he does not use this to his advantage.

The watch on my mother's wrist
Is ticking away the time
Not really caring about family problems
As the table does.
He just ticks on all day
and every day.

My mother takes great care of him
As he is the very first watch
That my mother received.
But he has gone on ticking
Through the years and
I am sure he has seen
Much
Of the family history.

And of course, even maybe
Before my mother's wrist became his home
If he could talk I'm sure
Many unknown tales would have been revealed
Happy and sad.

He does not bother with the life around him.
He just makes sure he is on time
And of course
The time on the face of him
Is completely to his mind and not to anyone else.

Sally had the table's intuitive attitude – straight and erect, yet knowing and caring about the family. She also needed the detachment of her mother's watch, to mark the present from the past that was 'to his mind and not to anyone else'.

I think that this echoes Freud's insight into the timeless quality of primary loss:

> An infant at the breast does not as yet distinguish his ego from the external world as the source of the sensations flowing in upon him. He gradually learns to do so, in response to various prompting. He must be very strongly impressed by the fact that some sources of excitation, which he will later recognize as his own bodily organs, can provide him with sensations at any moment, whereas other sources evade him from time to time – and only reappear as a result of his screaming for help. In this way there is *for the first time* set over against the ego an 'object' which is only forced to appear by a special action.
>
> (Freud 1963: 4; emphasis added)

STYLES IN THE THERAPEUTIC REGRESSIONS

Both Frank and Sally responded hyperactively at first, which I under-valued, seeing it as a simple release of creative initiative and not realizing the element of defensiveness in such a response, because the images were contained in a traditional art style. Sally covered the table with recog-nizable objects until, amongst their profusion emerged the vital shapes of a mother and child. Frank's traditional drawings came easily to him until one of them showed a derelict house with a notice-board, 'Keep out', that indicated a hidden problem he was not ready to face.

At first Sally's little figures were scattered over the work table in a way that later seemed to dismantle their meaning as a resistance to conscious thought, but when she grouped them and made them talk about each other they revealed her sensitivity to relationships, and, as the little images developed 'speaking parts' in the second group of mother and child, Sally was able to reach the intensity of her traumatic experi-ence.

It was essential that I should do nothing to show my appreciation of their ability to create naturalistic images, for this might well confine the children to their rational attitude and block their need for therapeutic regression.

Sally's use of the images in joint play with me was very precarious; her self-esteem might have anchored her feelings to the intuitive/perceptive attitude if this had seemed mutually gratifying, and Frank's ability to use Traditional naturalism implied detachment, distancing the images by a mood of reticence and intuitive perception. This attitude enabled him to make rather sophisticated drawings that were unexpected, coming as they did from a tough-looking little country boy who had sudden, irrational outbursts of panic.

The symbolism of creative art – the 'and – and – and' of visual imagery – contains feelings and ideas that are not consciously connected, and for both Sally and Frank this eventually extended their habitual attitude so that new associations occurred and each in different ways made a therapeutic regression to Archaic art.

WORDS AND POETRY

When Frank was able to think he became deeply depressed and only communicated through black paintings. The studio seemed safe enough to hold this sadness and when he began at last to speak about his bereavement he spoke simply and directly about his little brother and gave different versions of his death. I thought that he was confused rather than dissociated, for he responded directly to my suggestion that his social worker could help him to find out the true facts. His art remained dominantly Archaic, clinging to the symbolism of ships; these seemed a means to contain him and they comforted him.

Sally used words freely to allow her feelings to be expressed through the mouths of her images. These words were poetic, that is, to say that they went beyond her habitual way of thinking and flowed by free association to the images.

Many children's creativity moves freely between the media offered; clay can be used as paint, paint added to clay, stories or poems to pictures or claywork; words as titles or 'bubbles' of speech can add explicit meaning to an image, as in Jennie's painting *A Girl Lost in the Forest* (Figure 8.3). Poetry is a natural way for children to articulate; they may dictate a poem if someone is there to listen and write or, like Pat, they may write for themselves. Some children chant or say words that may come so thick and fast that they cannot spare the time to write them down or they may be too young to write. Once children can use words at all they use them to discover themselves. Here is a poem by a four-year-old girl dealing with the birth of a brother:

I had a little doll
And it did like me
and it did love me
and it was lovely.

It had a pink dress
And three little babies
she brought with her.

You could put them in
and take them out.

Because she was so lovely
She liked me and I kissed her
She lived in the toy cupboard
And her mother kept taking her out.
She kept walking out
And went to the shops
And said
'I want some petticoats'.

It is not difficult to interpret the poem; the past tense indicates a bereavement. However, poetry is more than a story told rhythmically; it is a means of linking past to present, known to unknown feeling. The art form creates the thought and extends it beyond literal interpretation.

A work of art has to be seen to be believed: it is not enough to describe it – this fragments it and destroys its living potential. Children even younger than the four-year-old poet know the value of their art, but they need some trusted person to help and appreciate the creation. This is not to overlook the fact that some children are too ill to be freely creative and the therapist must play into the situation in some way. Such interventions may not be art or therapy, they can be a means of affirming the mental space where play can begin.

An eleven-year-old autistic boy had the speech ability of a two-year-old but could use numbers symbolically. However, when he was upset these seemed sometimes to fragment his thoughts. The following incident illustrates the barren limits of this form of communication and my own effort to link it to a present loss.

Don was upset by his mother's absence and could not paint or draw so we counted the numbers on playing cards and then he wrote longer and longer columns of numbers that in every case he totalled as three. This did not relieve his panic at all so I said:

'Three is the number of your family. Mummy, Daddy and Don. Three people in your home. When Mummy is on holiday. Now there are two people in your home.'

Donald moaned and shouted, 'No more. No more!', his eyes filling with tears.

I said, 'Mummy is one of your family. When she is out of the house she is still Don's Mummy, Don's family. Daddy is one, Mummy is one, Don is one. That is three. Three ones are three, as you know.'

'No more Mrs Jones!' cried Don, speaking of a neighbour.

'Mrs Jones is not part of Don's family; Mrs Jones goes home to her family. Mummy is Don's family when she is on holiday, when she is here with Mrs Simon and Don, when she is at home.'

Donald remembered this conversation and referred to it many times by drawing large figure threes and asking 'Mrs Jones?'

A 'highly defended' teenager handed me a poem on crumpled paper; it allowed the expression and sharing of feelings that he could not voice in any other way:

GHOSTS

Ghosts crowd round my beaten head,
Grab me, "We are dead"
"Why didn't your heart break before?"
"Is this sorrow the last straw?"
"The last stone and final blow?"
"And where we went you must go?"

Depression and even suicidal feelings can be shaped into a poem and shared in such protective containers; then there is less need to act out, as Sally, Frank and other grief-stricken children have shown.

Consider the following bereavement poem. It mirrors an adolescent boy's mental state and brings the heart of the matter to the fore. Through the poem he tells himself why he has to kick:

I kick old stones along the ground
I kick old bones when they are found.
I kicked the cat when it was dead
I kicked the bucket, full of lead.
Then I went and kicked my head.

Another adolescent wrote:

ANTICIPATION OF REMOVAL

My senses form a nicotine
Confusion – exit space and time.
No existence of my kind
End of the world already signed
Seat of conscience undermined
The furthermost thought confined
Within the skull, within the mind
A Predominant thought: to find
The reason WHY.

CONCLUSION

Bereavement is seen as having two levels for some adults and children. The immediate loss may reflect primary bereavement that could only be experienced somatically at the time of infancy. This trauma may only be resolved through a symbolic equivalent in a later loss.

Bereavement is an experience of being robbed, deprived and left desolate that is normally dealt with in states of forgetting and remembering the loss; but primary bereavement seems to attach a sense of ongoing reality, reflecting a time when bereavement was met before the infant or young child could use words or associations that allow experience to be recollected. This is the primary shock that can only be assimilated through replication in a later bereavement.

Therapy requires sufficient time for symbolic re-enactment in created art objects worked through in fear, grief and outrage, before their integrative effect can be used.

SUMMARY

I have tried to distinguish the special qualities of creative art in therapy with children and young people who may not be aware of bereavement grief and anger at first. The concept of a primary bereavement is discussed and compared with other responses to bereavement that are worked through by alternately remembering and forgetting during a normal process of mourning.

Examples are given to show the importance of the provision of sufficient time for primary bereavement to be met and worked through in the containing symbolism of creative art.

REFERENCES

Balint, E. (1993) *Before I was I*, New York: Free Association Books.
Blake, W. (1939) *Poems and Prophesies*, London: J. M. Dent & Sons Ltd.
Freud, S. (1949) *The Ego and the Id*, London: Hogarth Press.
—— (1963) *Civilisation and its Discontents*, London: Hogarth Press.
Simon, R. M. (1991) *The Symbolism of Style*, London: Routledge.
Tustin, F. (1972) *Autism and Childhood Psychosis*, London: Hogarth Press.
Winnicott, D. W. (1971) *Playing and Reality*, London: Tavistock.

Chapter 9

Art therapy with a maltreated child

Sleep, Sleep! beauty bright
Dreaming o'er the joys of night.
Sleep, Sleep! in thy sleep
Little sorrows sit and weep.

Sweet Babe, in thy face
Soft desires I can trace,
Secret joys and secret smiles,
Little pretty infant wiles.

(*Cradle Song*, Blake 1939: 375)

Although the therapeutic work described here is with one particular child, it also touches on some general problems, such as the different and sometimes conflicting aims of therapy and interpretation, especially in cases where assessment is sought in order to clarify a legal issue.

The principle demonstrated by this case is that almost all patients will help themselves if the conditions are right. If they cannot help themselves, then a therapist cannot help them. This is not at all to say that the patient cannot be helped by someone or something else; in this case, enough had gone wrong to be put right.

When cases of child maltreatment or abuse come to public notice, intense emotions are stirred in all who work on the case or hear about it. Our sympathies reach out to the child by identification with our own, usually forgotten past, and our defences against pain at that time harden against the abuser. This subjective response is not the best way of helping a child for whom the incest barrier has in some way broken down. Therapy requires of us our concerned attention to the way that the individual child has dealt with what has happened: work with *that* is essential if the child is to recover fully.

I have her permission to describe art therapy with an eleven-year-old girl taken into care as a suspected victim of incest. At one stage there was some expectation in the Social Services that art therapy would clarify or confirm the facts, but her social worker's main concern was for therapeutic help, and she arranged for me to provide individual sessions of one hour a week, continuing for two years.

THE CASE

I will call the pretty, radiantly healthy eleven-year-old Boots, for when I first met her she continually drew attention to her feet, clad in boy's heavy, black shoes. Her manner was charming and cajoling: it had been described as 'sexually precocious' but to me it had the sensuous appeal of a much younger, cuddly child. However, having summed up the situation as 'harmless', Boots did not waste much time on me but immediately started to use paint, clay or the writing materials, needing no help or direction for any of them. The art material to hand released her need to create self-images in various ways. While working, she was intensely absorbed, but before and afterwards she affected the manner of a bland, carefree and self-admiring child.

An early session illustrates the difference between this surface and her submersion in creative reverie. The poem below accompanied a coloured sketch of fishes using blue paper as a background. The spelling and punctuation in this and all other poems given in the text are her own, excepting one which she dictated, to be discussed later.

THE SCENE OF THE SEA

The boat under the water
The fish under the water
The seaweed under
The water
And the sand
Under the water.

Curly, whirly seaweed
Up high, tall and green.
The little red fish darts
Into the boat.

Rough, rough water
Swirls the fish around.
Poor little fish.
You'd better wag your tail.*

*This line of the poem was first altered to 'you'd better swim well' and then altered again to the original.

Two green fish,
Swimming past the boat
See the other fish
Inside the boat.

They swim on past,
Swimming very fast,
They've seen a big shark
And hide behind the seaweed.

The yellow fish does see
The smaller little fish
He chases it round and round
But he cannot catch it.

Boots smiled at me as she pointed out that the little fish was red and different from the other fish. She told me that she loved swimming and had often been taken to the swimming baths by her father; it seemed that the symbolism of the work became conscious to her as she showed me the poem, and she expected me to understand it. We talked a bit about the little red fish's feelings – whether it would be frightened: Boots thought that it was red and flustered.

In the first weeks of therapy it was difficult to imagine this charming young girl, a picture of glowing health, as a maltreated child; only through her paintings and poems could I see that she was confused about her identity. She seemed to assume femininity while inwardly maintaining male identification, perhaps even to a delusional extent. Young girls may envy the satisfactions of being a boy, idealizing male independence and power, but Boots seemed to feel that she *was* a valiant boy and this blocked any identification with her mother.

Her art style gave me further concern. As discussed in the introductory chapter and in my previous book, *The Symbolism of Style* (1991) the way a picture is painted or a model is made in clay indicates the artist's unconscious attitude to the image that is made. This attitude may be a temporary or habitual way of seeing life.

In the first months of her work, Boots's art style was Archaic Linear; she usually drew large, childlike shapes as if they were flat, spaceless silhouettes, and when using clay she flattened it and drew an image on it with a pencil.

I understand this Archaic Linear style to express the dominance of sensuous reality over emotion, intuition and thought. This state of mind is seen in the behaviour of babies and very young children, but the style is also found in some adults who have regressed to sensuous dependence or schizophrenic thinking. Artists, such as Paul Klee may develop the capacity for such aesthetic regression elevated to a personal style, and it is found to dominate Archaic arts. As I illustrated in the introductory chapter, small children usually combine linear shapes with scribbled masses, if the art material permits.

Boots seemed quite indifferent to her removal into care – in a voice both self-satisfied and bland, she informed me, 'if I spill things I mop them up', but in the months that followed, the content of her art began to indicate sexual concerns. One day she rolled out a panel of clay and drew round the imprint of her hand, painting red finger-nails, and a widely grinning face on the palm. Behind this panel she placed a roll of clay, bent into a curving shape. She smiled at me confidingly and said it was a prop. This led me to ask her if she knew the saying 'I'm holding someone in the palm of my hand'. Boots hung her head and I felt that my remark had been intrusive.

One day she flattened a piece of clay and incised a silhouette of a horse in her usual, Archaic Linear style. Then, to my surprise, she stood it up and worked over it steadily for most of the hour, using the tips of her fingers with unusually tentative movements until she had made a three-dimensional model of a horse and rider. She asked me how the clay could be made to stand and I suggested that she set it on a base. She used this idea immediately, making the base a very deep pedestal, painting it black, adding some stones in front of the horse's feet and finally adding her name to a side panel.

This was the first time I had seen Boots work methodically, searching out a modelling tool and using it to achieve precise details. At one point she changed the little figure of the rider from a man to a girl with a long rope of black hair down her back.

Boots's mood was so untypical that I felt the importance of the object that she had created. There seemed no doubt that she had envisaged herself as a girl who could master the huge horse and make it jump the stones. It seemed that she had found a mood or rediscovered a trust in her feminine ability to deal with life, perhaps her sexual life. One model is only one mood, but it was very satisfying to her, and to me, that she could achieve it (Figure 9.1).

The style of this model, of Traditional Massive art, draws intui-tively upon visual perception, and its images are more naturalistic than the simple shapes that form Archaic art. External reality modifies the ele-mental intensity of emotion and sensuous feeling in a way that is not possible for the young child or an adult dominated by passion. The model showed me that Boots could use the outer world of shared reality even though she was still deeply confused about her identity, and the little image reflected an assurance of gender that I had not seen before.

Boots was delighted with her model; she painted it carefully and asked if she could take it to show her family. I thought the naturalism of this piece might encourage them to appreciate her latent ability and I agreed

Figure 9.1 Horse and Rider, Traditional Massive

that she could take it on her next visit. I was quite wrong in this: the result was a painful rejection. Boots said very little, only, 'I took it home but they didn't look at it much. They didn't seem to like it. I gave it to Daddy and the baby broke it. Daddy put it on the TV and he [the baby] took it, and you can't get anything away from him, he'd shout the house down.' It was the first time I had seen Boots's complacency disturbed. She did not speak about her mother's reaction to the model but soon after this Boots began to show emotional sensibility and a longing for nurturing parents. This poem reveals her need:

THE MUMMY AND BABY SUNFLOWER

'Oh Mummy, can I ask you this
why do we need the sun to grow?'

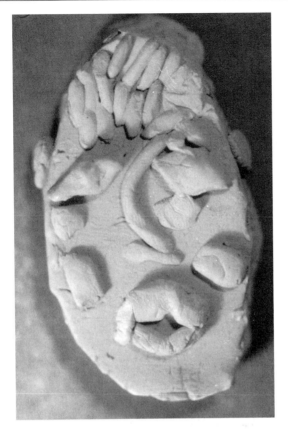

Figure 9.2 Crying Face, Linear transition

'As our names are sunflowers
God made us to be tall.
That's why we've got the sun
to make us tall and bright.'

This shows Boots's attempts to see herself as a little daughter, but her mother was too upset and accused Boots of enjoying the pain she caused, coming between her parents and breaking up the marriage.

As Boots became more aware of her past confusion of gender identity she recalled a time when she had been taken to see Father Christmas: 'He said, "Here's a nice little lad," and I said, "I'm not a lad, I'm a boy." Wasn't that funny?'

In her first months of work with me, Boots had seemed untroubled by her removal into care but now she began to realize how traumatic this experience had been. She told me that she did not know how long she

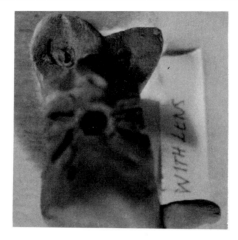

Figure 9.3 Push-me, Archaic Massive

had been in the children's home and described a continuing sense of confusion about time: 'Its nearly my birthday ... not really ... They say its
nearly Christmas and it seems like Christmas was yesterday. Its weird.'

The situation deteriorated and Boots returned from her home visits
angry and disturbed. She misbehaved in the residential home, organizing
sexual games with other children and falling into tantrums that alienated
the staff, who sometimes felt she was out of control. On one occasion
there was a violent incident in which she was hit and put under a cold
shower. She cried when telling me of this, her cheerful invulnerability
broken down.

Of the tantrums, she said, 'Mummy makes me have them.' She rolled
out a circular disc in clay and incised a cross in it asking 'Is this the cross
of Jesus? My eyes are watering.' Figure 9.2, *Crying Face*, is a bas-relief
she made at that time in the Archaic Massive style.

Here is a story she wrote that illustrates an aspect of her problem of
identity and her parents' inability to recognize her as an individual:

> Once upon a time there was a lovely girl called Kelly, so one day her
> Mummy and Daddy decided to buy her a swing but there was only one
> thing wrong. it was too small for her. They thought she was smaller
> than she was. She had better fun running round it so she found a ball
> in the grass and she had good fun bouncing the ball. The swing she
> gave to another girl and told her parents so they bought her a bat
> instead, as she had the ball. That was wrong too.

In this state of regression Boots made images of her sense of confused
identity when she modelled a mummy and baby duck in clay, adding a

third, strange creature she called an 'owlcat' with a hole in its middle. Boots said sadly 'Its name is Push-me and it doesn't belong to the ducks' (Figure 9.3).

One day she painted a large picture of a room in a childlike, Archaic style. The walls and ceiling were coloured a violent pink and the furniture was indicated in black. A black cat was shown, sitting on a blue and white rug. The colours and scattered details suggested that this painting showed a world of sensuous and emotional reality filled with disconnected objects. She was deeply absorbed by this picture but did not seem distressed by it at the time; however, the following week she wrote a poem that obviously referred to the painting as an intensely disturbing experience:

THE CAT

A lonesome cat crawled by the room
and sat down by the fire,
On such a sunny, warm day
He didn't care how warm he was.

A room so pretty he must have thought
Would tire the old cat down.
But he sat on top of me
And squeezed my fur in tight.

I tried to be as comfortable
as if I was in bed
My fur gave way and I colappessed
It was the old cat's fault.

A blazing fire.
A black old cat.
A carpet white and blue.
You squashed my fur and now I'm dead.

"I'm sorry sorry sorry
For killing you on this fine day.
I'll get back off your blue fur
And maybe you'll be well again."

I'm well again O little cat
I hope you understood
That when you sit on top of me
You know I will collapps.

"I am the cat and I am sad
I'll go off in a huff
and don't you worry, you furry carpet,

I won't, I won't I won't squash you
'til your dead."

This poem, together with Boots's distress, gave me such concern that I felt I must share it with her social worker. Although the poem could be read as an allegory, it also appeared to describe a mood of psychic disintegration and physical assault. By showing the poem to the social worker I was relieved of the pressure upon me to discover how far it might refer to actual reality. I also agreed that it could be produced at a case discussion, a further breach of confidentiality that I hoped was justified by Boots's need to continue art therapy. Although I deeply regret my use of this poem to buy more therapeutic time, in the work setting at that time art therapy was generally seen as a brief intervention, to be terminated if deemed unproductive by the Social Services.

Boots was clearly intelligent enough to cope with normal secondary education but her behaviour continued to be very disturbed. Although she remained friendly to me she suffered outbursts of rage and destructiveness elsewhere. I believe that she might well have included me as an object of her anger if she had not invested so much in her art. Her painting, claywork and particularly her poetry, were too precious an outlet for her to endanger. Only in art therapy was she able to express and contain the outrage that denial of her identity had blocked her out of her thinking and feeling Self for so many years, leaving only the sensuous and sexual persona.

As the months passed, Boots gave up her false identity, a combination of whore and feckless boy. Without that mask, her suffering was visible in her face and her mother could not ignore it. Boots was no longer a healthy child but pale, sleepless and generally ill. At last her mother made efforts to overcome her jealousy and to protect her, but these efforts remained ambivalent. Meanwhile, as her daughter gave up her delusion of imperviousness she gained deeper insight into the role she had adopted, that her parents had assigned to her. One day, when she had been mindlessly playing with some clay, she said that it looked like a boot. This image held her attention for some time until it seemed to flood her with sexual excitement. In her need to give meaning to this shape she was able to contain her feelings in a poem that I wrote at her dictation:

THE BOOT

If a boot were as big as a grandfather's 'clock'
What would a boot be like?
But if it was as big as me
I would say it would fit a giant.

I am a boot and I am not big
But I can admit to fat;
The person who gets their foot into me
Must be a chubby woman, or man.

So if you go out and notice a boot
That's maybe as tall as you,
Don't worry yourself, you can think of me
And look so funny with me on.

This savage poem reflects the experience of being made to feel as worthless as an old boot. The image of the owlcat – a strange little subhuman animal – seems transferred to a monstrous, life-sized boot. I was troubled by my need to comfort her and my continuing conviction that no one could do this successfully except Boots herself.

Throughout this time her art continued to show a tormented struggle to integrate the opposing realities of her inner and outer life by allowing both to exist within the frame of art. Her poems and pictures helped her to contain the extremes of her chaotic feelings. It was very painful to see her struggles and difficult to refrain from interfering, questioning her about the images and challenging her reticence, but she did not speak directly about them or give any sign that she would welcome or even tolerate any attempt to share my understanding of her symbolism. Such was the way she had chosen to communicate and its integrative power would be destroyed if I had approached the subject directly. Moreover, if I had acquired information that she had not given freely, I would have had to report to her social worker and Boots would have been forced to give evidence before the courts. This could have been another trauma, for I sensed love and compassion for the 'old cat' in her poem; the relation between the cat and the blue rug was extremely complex. Could I force Boots to look only on the sexual abuse and maltreatment in a public denunciation while she was working through love, anger and intense, tormenting disappointment? I felt I could not.

Her trust in the unspoken alliance, through art therapy, that she felt with me is illustrated in the next poem, which she wrote at the end of a session that had been briefly interrupted by a telephone call:

Ting, ting a ling. that's the telephone
Ting ting a ling just when in alone.
Hello Hello who are you
Oh i'm Mrs Simon.
Oh how do you do?
I say is Mum at home.
Not in sorry shes not in yet
I would say she would be back at four

OK By
By
Oh do feel grown-up alone
chatting on
the telephone.

I saw in this poem the dual need for contact and distance that she resented and yet needed for our communication. Boots needed to envisage herself as a powerful 'Mum' who was not always available if I, in role-reverse, should call. Also, there was perhaps some fear that I might ring her mother and conspire with her.

This use of an actual incident for a symbolic image seemed a step towards integration, a new ability to imbue external life with symbolic meaning – a move that she had so briefly discovered in the horse and rider.

At last Boots was able to write directly about her deep distress and find some sympathetic acknowledgement within her family in her brother. As often before, she found a foothold in writing a poem in which she recognized that one of her family was able to see her as she was, and share some sense of mutual identification. This was an extremely important discovery for Boots.

The poem mirrors the spontaneous process of creative art that draws incoherent feelings into a containing frame. Her emotion is reflected in the misspelling of 'know' and the small 'i' in the second line, but she corrected these when the poem's message became conscious by reiteration and the poem was able to 'speak' of the idea of her brother's hidden sympathy.

Its funny my brother now just how I feel
When i'm grumpy! he slumpy and gives me his eyes.
Its funny my brother knows just how I feel
When I was a crying he came by my side
And all that he thought of was to sit down and laugh.
Its funny my brother knows just how I feel.

The poem shows a moment when she broke her false self-image of imperviousness and appreciated her brother's ambiguous reaction. In this poem Boots showed her understanding of her brother's inability to show his feelings, as she herself had suffered as 'a boy'; now she was able to cry as a girl, without disguise.

As Boots began to respond as a sister to her brother rather than competing with him as one boy to another, she faced the impossibility of making any change at all in her place in the family. This was extremely painful to her and, in the vulnerability of her newly awakened emotion, she wept as she painted a view of the family round the dinner table.

As time went on, Boots became more and more able to realize her grief and fury, and sometimes to hold her emotions within the strengthened ego of her gender identity. She showed this one day when doodling her initial, adding flowing hair to it. 'Now it's a she', she remarked. Her ego also contributed to her art, as it had when she had created *Horse and Rider*; now it moved freely between Archaic and Traditional styles, showing that she was in touch with both inner and outer realities, although the two were still separated as disconnected moods.

Erratic changes of mood are a feature of adolescence and their occasional integration was an important stage in her therapy. For example, Boots used the proportions of a Traditional Linear figure to represent 'an ugly girl in spectacles' called *Emily*; then, the following week *Emily* was worked over, shortened and remade as an Archaic Massive image of a little child about two years old, dressed in a patterned nightgown. The pattern was made by incising the clay with a pencil forced in with punishing jabs and cuts. I wondered to myself if these represented an attack on her skin's sensuousness. The figure held a tiny mug in one hand and a biscuit in the other (Figure 9.4). 'Poor little thing', said Boots sadly as she repeatedly thrust the pencil into the space between Emily's feet.

One day Boots made a small pot, very carefully using coils of clay in the way she had been taught to do at school. Inside the pot she set even tinier coils which she described as 'shells containing pearls and stones, and a snake or two, turned into flowers'.

This little bowl became exceptionally important to her. The complexity of its symbolic image and its contents seemed to be directed towards her need to make a container for good and bad images. The symbolism of stones and snakes, pearls and flowers suggested that opposites were being held together. For the first time since she had made *Horse and Rider* she completed a work in small scale with the tips of her fingers, finally painting the pot inside and out. The style seemed transitional, lying between Traditional and Archaic, for the little coils had made the pot in a traditional way but the contents did not visually represent flowers or snakes. It might be said that the symbolism of the inner, Archaic world of little identical coils was being contained in the structure of outer reality.

As she was painting the little pot she said, 'Black is my favourite colour, I love black. I saw it on an envelope once.' I said that this envelope might have been a mourning letter that people used to send when there had been a death. Boots stared at her work for a while and then she wrote 'There was' on a piece of scrap paper. She carefully rearranged the contents of the pot several times, then her quiet mood changed and she told me that her grandfather had died, adding that she did not mind that, but from the tone of her voice it seemed that she was also speaking of a

Figure 9.4 Emily, Archaic Massive

psychic death that she herself was suffering. I felt an intense weight of recollection in her posture as she hung over the little pot, repeatedly rearranging the tiny coils. At last she put the model on the table before her and wrote a poem:

A BOWL

I found a bowl beside a hole
That looked to me so very old
That bowl beside that little hole
I thought it was two years old.

But when I looked that small bowl
I soon a glimpse of a tiny snake
It made me shriek and I broke that bowl
That looked like two years old to me.

And now that bowl is lying down,
Cracked to pieces in the ground
And I'll go and leave it
That bowl that looked like two years old.

TERMINATION

It is quite usual for a child be withdrawn from therapy as soon as the stage of acting out has given way to suppression. Therefore, as Boots was no longer misbehaving, the Social Services pressed for an early termination of her therapy; she was passing the age limit for the children's home and a new placement had to be found for her.

We had only a few weeks to prepare for termination, and in her final session she hid her face and was sullen and angry. I did ask if she was angry with me for seeming to give her up, but she did not answer; however, she responded indirectly by suggesting that we could both paint on the same piece of paper for once. Then she changed her mind, saying that she would rather 'make my childish drawings'.

Using paint, she rapidly drew on white paper in the transitional Linear style; the style informed me that she was preoccupied by incoherent feelings aroused as she sought expression of her thoughts. Her deliberate efforts allowed me to approach this drawing directly and tell Boots that I did not know what it meant but I had the idea that it was clear to her. She said 'I'll show you from the beginning' and numbered the drawings as a sequence. The drawing has been lost; perhaps she destroyed it; however Figure 9.5 is a sketch I made directly after the session and kept with my notes.

Boots was clearly distressed and seemed on the verge of an outburst of feeling. However, she took a small piece of paper and some paint and began drawing fragmentary shapes. She studied these intently and then numbered each fragment on another piece of paper and wrote:

One, Cheeks, no mouth [Actually she had drawn in a mouth].
Two, brown and red tears.
Three, blue.
Four, fire in a pot and a ghost coming into the fire – a ghost can
    do anything.
Six, brown hate zigzag.

Figure 9.5 My sketch of Boots's last painting

Seven, bag of rage must burst and burst the pot. Trouble begins.
Painted my green [actually blue] figure brown but now, oh
dear, his face has gone.
Eight, Fright. Man and ghost, no mouth.
Eight, Black line, black heart
and the end of it all is . . .

Round the blackened red heart Boots wrote 'FRIENDSHIP'.

Throughout this session I could follow the progress of her thought as it moved from her need to bond with me by sharing a painting, to independent expression of her chaotic 'childish' feelings.

Contemplating this painting, her mood changed again from free expression to verbal communication and then self-control when she said, 'I'll show you from the beginning', numbering the drawing and thereby introducing sequential order to the random images. Boots then made further efforts to understand and deal with her feelings in the work she entitled 'A Poem, Anger!', her signature claiming the authenticity of the poem carefully composed of numbered verses and decorated with flowers and heart shapes.

A POEM, ANGER!

1
Here am I alone, afraid
Although my friends and enemies sit
with me on the pages of life.
You may think it looks a messy page
But its MEANING! TRUE! if you understand.

2
Theres GHOSTS, they moan SPREADING!
through your body like paper
set on fire.
Trying to ANNOY! you, and get
you in a pretty well DISASTER.

3
But then again a red HEART!
you see, is trying to CONTROL you
You should listen well and take a heed
Of what its trying to say.

4
So you should UNDERSTAND! the
page right now.
And THINK! it for your self
But if this thing will give
you now
An idea of the painting.

There is no doubt in my mind that the sketch was made as an attempt to review her disturbing recollections before me; listing them showed her desire to set her feelings in an orderly sequence, a courageous attempt to share and contain their pain and complete her work with me.

I understood her suggestion that we paint together, and her withdrawal of this idea and the process of taking responsibility for herself. I understood self-permission in her temporary regression, described as 'my childish drawings', in the fragmented sketch that brings the Archaic, inner world to consciousness, showing how deeply she was trying to understand herself and control her feelings.

DISCUSSION

I hope that by exposing one particular child's suffering I have been able to indicate the importance of looking at child maltreatment as far more complex than it would appear in its purely legal aspect. There is a need to provide conditions in which the child feels safe enough to look very deeply at the mad way the family lived and how they are now dealing with their pain. Such work takes a long time and must be conducted by a therapist who is altogether non-judgemental. We must not invite the child to escape responsibility by blaming the adult or adults, nor must we be led into the fallacy that children are innocent, if this is taken to mean that they are ignorant of sensuous life and sexual excitements. We must not forget that their situation has arisen through a general failure in the whole family structure; to forget these things would be a dreadful injustice, denying the child access to his or her feelings of guilt, love, sorrow and pity that must be fully realized before the child is free to achieve truly adult life.

Therapy is not retributive: if a child's psychic development has been blocked and twisted, punishment of the offender will not remove the distortion or the block but can deflect the child's proper understanding by a misguided attempt to absolve him or her from all responsibility for any part in the tragedy; if this cannot be admitted it may permanently damage the child through dread of suspended punishment and possibly giving rise to repetition compulsion.

Given a full therapeutic opportunity, children like Boots can create images of their need to understand what has happened to them and use their creative initiative to discover and unravel the confusion they suffer.

THE SYMBOLIC IMAGERY OF *HORSE AND RIDER*

Under the term 'Phantasy', Freud and others have studied hidden wishes in works of art. Boots first created an image of male dominance in her model of the horse and rider but, as she worked on it, the figure was changed to a girl. In psychoanalytic terms this might well indicate the development from phallic to genital sexuality that enabled her to realize herself as truly feminine. If this had become conscious it would be no wonder that she asked for help, displacing her need upon the little model. Although I did not understand the full significance of this, her first plea for help, I sensed its importance. I knew that Boots was quite capable of inventing a way to support the horse but wanted to involve me in it for some reason, so I suggested that she make a clay 'ground' for it to stand on. She elaborated this notion to a pedestal that she decorated and signed, then carefully coloured the whole model in black, white and red.

Horse and Rider can be seen as a therapeutic 'progression in service of ego' but Boots also made a 'regression in service of ego' (Kris 1971: 177) when the figure *Emily* was changed from a Traditional Linear image to an Archaic Massive model, with Boots showing love and pity for 'the poor little thing!'

The power of art to transcend the split between inner and outer reality can be studied in detail in Boots's poetry. In one instance the process is illuminated by the preparatory work that formed a little clay bowl. Perhaps Boots started to make a conventional pot – a piece of coiled pottery that could win marks at school for its neat conformity – for she made several coils before becoming absorbed in reverie. Then the coils were used to form a circular container for other Circles, little coils that she called 'flowers' and 'snakes' but that were not given attributes or any representation. These tiny, abstract circles appear to symbolize good and bad things inside her, pearls and flowers, stones and snakes.

The claywork led her to write a poem about another bowl, and as we follow the visual links between coils and snakes, pearls and stones, the poetic image is also used as a container. Then her sensuous pleasure in making a pot from coils like snakes connected with an early sensuous experience that had been traumatic.

Boots continued her integrative impulse to use words as a container by writing down her response to my remark about black-edged envelopes.

BOOTS'S ART STYLES

Art styles reflect the attitude taken towards the content of an art work. They are primarily based on the need to relate Self and Other in the symbolic shape of a Circle in a Square. Boots's first style showed this primary need as Archaic Linear art that later acquired attributes of emotional reality seen in the *Push-me* and *Emily* figures.

Horse and Rider gave a glimpse of Boots' potential for intuitive responsiveness, but when Boots reverted to the Archaic mode it developed towards a Massive style in the transitional image of the crying face. She was able to express her emotional deprivation fully in *Emily*, a full-length figure as a child holding a tiny cup in its hand.

When I first met Boots she seemed morally asleep, out of touch with the emotional implications of her removal to the children's home. This massive dissociation endangered her reason, but she showed a need to 'wake' by the creative initiative she used in her painting, claywork and poems. In these ways she worked through her confused sense of identity and came to know herself as a separate, discerning individual.

Boots came to therapy having lost touch with her true identity. Unsure whether she was in one year or the next, whether she was a girl or boy, she seemed to exist in the timeless present of sensuous reality and her sensuous appeal probably seemed her only hold on life.

In paint, clay and poetry Boots found insight and a need to claim and defend herself. Her symbolic images shaped her deepest feelings while protecting the privacy she demanded.

Psychotherapy is not making clever and apt interpretations; by and
large it is a long-term giving the patient back what the patient brings.
It is a complex derivative of the face that reflects what is there to be
seen. I like to think of my work this way, and to think that if I do this
well enough the patient will find his or her own self, and to be able to
exist and to feel real. Feeling real is more than existing; it is finding a
way to exist as oneself, and to relate to objects as oneself, and to have
a self into which to retreat for relaxation. But I would not like to give
the impression that I think this task of reflecting what the patient brings
is easy. It is not easy, and it is emotionally exhausting.

(Winnicott 1971: 117)

Boots's art was therapy, not evidence; it neither proved nor disproved
the possibility of criminal injustice. Although her therapy was cut short,
I was hopeful that this very intelligent girl would continue to 'feel real'
and make positive use of what life offered. Two years after the end of
her therapy she made a brief social call at my home and, as she was
leaving, I was pleased to share a friendly hug of farewell. In adult life
Boots has found herself as a loving wife and mother.

I commenced this chapter with two verses from Blake's *Cradle Song*
that illuminate the sensuous life that sleeps in the little child. Now I will
complete the poem, that speaks so simply for Boots of the emotional
storms and stresses that invade sensuous life when it awakes:

As thy softest limbs I feel,
Smiles as of the morning steal
O'er thy cheek, & o'er thy breast
Where thy little heart does rest.

O! the cunning wiles that creep
In thy little heart asleep!
When thy little heart does wake
Then the dreadful lightnings break.

From thy cheek & from thy eye,
O'er the youthful harvests nigh,
Infant wiles & infant smiles
Heaven and earth of peace beguiles.

(*Cradle Song*, Blake 1939: 375)

SUMMARY

Maltreatment of any sort damages or fragments a child's self-identity
through the violence of adult sensuous or emotional demands, and
any therapeutic intervention must avoid further psychic destruction.

Undirected art therapy can provide a benign situation in which a child can act, feel, think, and say or not say whatever is needed for self-evaluation.

This case illustrates the way one young girl's creative art dealt with numerous offences made against her. The stages of her recovery are reflected in the style and content of her paintings, sculpture and poetry.

REFERENCES

Blake, W. (1939) *Poems and Prophesies*, London: J. M. Dent & Sons Ltd.
Freud, S. (1961) *Introductory Lectures on Psycho-analysis*, London: Allen & Unwin.
Kris, E. (1971) *Psychoanalytic Explanations in Art*, New York: Schocken.
Winnicott, D. W. (1971) *Playing and Reality*, London: Tavistock.

Chapter 10

Research into styles in art

THE PICTORIAL STYLES OF PRIMARY SCHOOL CHILDREN

The art therapist's task is to understand the symbolic meaning of patients' art styles, content and anything that is said during a session. Such concentrated attention to an individual needs to be counterbalanced in some way by a wider view of the general procedure, that may be spaced over several years. Comparisons need to be made between a patient's past and present art styles by some form of visual aid, such as a graph. I think it is also important that I keep in mind the spontaneous art of normal children who draw, paint and sometimes make things in clay and write poems.

Children are natural artists and all adults have been children, but adults are less inclined to make images spontaneously, unless they doodle or come to art therapy. Some years ago I had an opportunity to collect 23 drawings made by first-year university students playing a party game of 'Draw your Partner'. There I found examples of all eight styles.

A PILOT STUDY

I offer the little I have done systematically to study this area and I must leave it to others to take up the challenge that it presents.

Starting from the observation that an artist's style can be recognized and classified according to four basic modes, a pilot study was undertaken to see whether children's art showed a similar constancy. Left to themselves some children make images of things seen or thought about, while others of the same age seem happy to use colour and line without trying to represent anything. Age and maturity come in to this; younger children are more likely to make non-representational pictures than the older ones. Excep-tions are always to be found and one remarkable example of Traditional Massive art by a four-year-old child was published by Lorna Selfe (1977).

I had two aims. I wanted to know how many styles I would find in a large number of school children. I also wondered if the subject matter would influence the pictorial style used.

I hoped to elicit the styles through four set subjects, and chose four that were often used by children at that time. The King and House subjects were expected to elicit an Archaic style while the Landscape and Interior more objective, Traditional images. Each child's treatment of these subjects, the choice and handling of an art material, the scale and colour/tone would be studied.

The King subject was chosen to typify a superior being such as Superman, a giant, prehistoric monster, pop star or Popeye. The House subject might recall an actual home or an invented one. Similarly, the Landscape might be remembered or made up while an Interior could be inside anything.

I was very fortunate in finding teachers who were also interested in child art and would administer the small pilot study I had devised.

METHOD

Fifty children aged between nine and eleven years from two classes in a mixed primary school in London and in Belfast were invited to complete four subjects, one each week in the usual classroom conditions. The drawing paper was standard white cartridge, 15 by 11½ inches, and the class teacher asked the children to start each subject by drawing a frame the size and shape they wanted to fill. They were given a choice of poster paint, felt-tipped pens, wax crayons and pencils. Of the hundred children participating, 80 completed all four subjects, 320 in all.

First, the paintings were classified according to Table 10.1. Each work was assessed regardless of subject-matter, dividing the pictures into the basic groups of Archaic and Traditional styles; these were then subdivided by their Massive or Linear qualities. Paintings that contained elements of two styles were arranged in their respective Transitional style (see Glossary, page 186).

RESULTS

Various results emerged from this study.

A The four set subjects were seen to actively promote a style.
B The Archaic styles were markedly less than the Traditional, which was a generally expected result for children of this age range working in a classroom setting.
C The Archaic Linear style was only used for the King subject.
D 5 children confined themselves to a single style for all four subjects.

E   17 used one style three times.
F   48 used one style twice.
G   13 used a different style for each subject.
H   3 drawings were made in the transitional area between the Archaic
    and Traditional styles.

Table 10.1 Characteristics of styles

Name	Design	Visual effect
Archaic styles		
Linear	Symmetrical	Huge, awe-inspiring
Transitional	Diagonal	Chaotic
Massive	Convex	Emotional
Transitional	Anomalous	Metamorphic
Traditional styles		
Massive	Conventional	Intuitive/perceptive
Transitional	Ornamental	Superficial
Linear	Detailed	Thoughtful
Transitional	Fragmented	Allusive

Table 10.2 Proportion of styles used for each subject

	Archaic			Traditional				
Style	1	2	3	4	5	6	7	8
King	6	4	15	22	27	1	5	–
House	–	1	21	26	4	20	6	2
Landscape	–	–	1	40	30	6	2	1
Interior	–	1	7	25	6	18	22	1

Each style and each transitional style was used. This was mildly surprising. I had
expected to find that developmental progress in children of this age range would have
eliminated some Archaic styles.

Table 10.3 Subjects illustrated in the expected styles

Subject	Expected style	Actual number
King (style 1)	Archaic Linear style	6
House (style 3)	Archaic Massive style	21
Landscape (style 5)	Traditional Massive style	30
Interior (style 7)	Traditional Linear style	22

This suggests that art styles are influenced by personal and maturational effects rather
than a set subject.

Table 10.4 Proportion of styles used

Style	1	2	3	4	5	6	7	8
Totals	6	6	44	113	67	54	35	4

This shows substantial grouping around styles 3, 4, 5, 6, 7, with a peak at style 4.

OBSERVATIONS

Two of the results were outstanding – the domination of the Archaic Linear style for the King subject, and the prevalence of the Massive transitional style.

The Archaic Linear style is a sensuous reaction to a subject as huge and awe-inspiring; therefore it seemed that only six children in this age group responded to the sensuous aspect of reality, and then only in association with the idea of a King.

The transitional style lies between the two basic styles concerned with Massive form. They give an impression of metamorphosis, of grotesque, humorous or animistic attitudes to life. Typical of the latency response, it was used for nearly one-third of all paintings (113 in all).

METHOD

My interpretation is based on comparisons with art made in other settings – free painting by normal children at home and art therapy with troubled children.

The subject of a painting represents the painter's conscious intention and the style reflects assumptions about the subject. The child is identified with his work through the symbolism of his style. If this particular style is appreciated by others, such as a schoolteacher, parent or peer group, it can continue until it changes spontaneously, usually at the onset of puberty or secondary education.

Considered over the whole, the proportions of the children's art styles indicate a predominant preference for a blend of Archaic and Traditional art. The proportion of Archaic styles diminishes in relation to their distance from the central position, and fades into the Traditional styles.

Transitional styles suggest preoccupations with change, or dual points of view. In the Massive transitional style, this indicates moods shifting between the inner reality of sensuous and emotional life, and intuitive and conceptual versions of the outer world. This style integrates both aspects of reality at a time when the pressure of compulsory education and the child's growing self-awareness are coming into conflict.

CONCLUSIONS

The pilot study indicated that children 9–11 years old normally use both Archaic and Traditional art styles in their art work. Most of the children were influenced by the set subjects but some preference for a particular style was assumed when one style appeared in several subjects within the set.

NEW DIRECTIONS SUGGESTED

The results raised questions about the design of the study and the effect of its setting in formal class work. It would be interesting to look further into the relation of the subject to style – for example, the fact that only six children used the Archaic Linear style and then only for the King subject. The ages of the groups studied depended on the classroom setting and a further study that would narrow the spread to one year instead of the class average of three years might give a clearer picture of the use of art styles in normal maturation.

I would like to know more about the possible causes of preference for the Massive transitional style which links Archaic to Traditional art through the common use of mass. Archaic art presents mass as convexity, giving an illusion of heavy forms that seem to bulge forward from the picture plane and is associated in art therapy with emotional dominance, while Traditional Massive art gives an impression of receding space, an illusion of tunnelling back through the paper into the distance, implying a reticent or reflective attitude of mind. In transitional Massive art the effect of space is disjointed and this might reflect the normal process of maturation, when ego-centred needs are disturbed by external necessity.

It is possible that an habitual style reflects a fixation to one period of life when maturation was temporarily halted. The reason for this in normal children is not at all clear. I would not conclude automatically that a child in mainstream education who preferred to use an Archaic style in his eleventh year was suffering from mental illness.

A very brief example of the exclusive use of a style can be found in my experience of art therapy with two autistic boys whom I saw separately for some years. Both boys persisted with the Traditional Linear style. Although both could use Archaic Massive art, they clung to the extreme limitations of numerical figures when upset. I felt that these children depended on a mood that was as far as possible from emotional feelings, as if they could not tolerate the chaos of sensuous and emotional fusion we recognize in the Archaic transitional style.

SUMMARY

The basic styles of art present four different ways of comprehending life. A pilot study was set up to study the use of art at the end of latency. The results indicated that normal children of the nine to eleven age group use both subjective (Archaic) and objective (Traditional) images in response to given subjects. This observation is discussed in terms of the symbolism of the styles.

REFERENCES

Kris, E. (1971) *Psychoanalytic Explorations in Art*, New York: Schocken.
Selfe, L. (1977) *Nadia*, New York: Academic Press.
Simon, R. M. (1991) 'Pictorial Styles in the Art of Children', *British Journal of Aesthetics*, 16.3: 272–8.
—— (1991) *The Symbolism of Style*, London: Routledge.
Winnicott, D. W. (1971) *Playing and Reality*, London: Tavistock.

Conclusion

When I first admitted disturbed and ill adults to my studio in 1941 I was surprised by and envious of their imaginative freedom. Some worked unselfconsciously in a rather conventional style while others used simple, childlike images. Their work was quite different from the approaches either of sophisticated professionals or timid amateurs. I asked myself: 'What is going on that allows creative images to form so freely on paper and in clay when the professional finds creativity difficult and the amateur cannot be creative at all?'

I thought of Rousseau and his attack on education and began to think that 'knowledge puts the mind in chains'. Yet I knew it was simply not possible for me to forget my knowledge of art and rely upon the effect of ignorance. Certainly, I was ignorant of the effects of mental illness and knew myself to resist popular notions of mad people. It seemed best to cherish this ignorance while extending my knowledge of art styles in an unprejudiced way, as far as I could. I looked at the art styles that I had dismissed as 'bad' art. These turned out to be the styles of painting that were unfashionable at that time: for instance, the detailed and literal illustrations that won academic approval in the last century. These paintings seemed intended to make things look as people generally saw them, and they tended to represent trees and flowers and faces which were judged to be the proper subjects for painting. I could not dismiss this style, however, when I saw it appear from under a patient's hand, confidently delineated by someone who said they had never held a brush before. Why did someone paint in this way, or any other way? What was art? What was going on? Painters in this literal or factual style seem to see clearly the objects they depict in their mind's eye as an image to trace on the paper. William Blake drew a head of the ghost of a flea twice, so it was said, the second time because the flea had opened its mouth. Was this a hallucination or an unusual form of recollection – how could he have seen the mouth of the flea, let alone the ghost of its mouth?

Other patients approached art in a vague, scribbly way, seeming to have no object in mind; they seemed to play about in a dreamy way, smearing paint or scribbling with little broken lines or washes of colour giving a faint impression of blurred shapes until, as they said, 'something came to them'. Such drawings or paintings were not planned, clear ideas that could be outlines, but impressions of objects in space and light, casting shadows, of one thing belonging to another, affecting it and being affected in turn.

Then there was the other sort of art altogether; drawings, paintings and clay images that had tremendous force in their simple symmetry or large areas of colour; this was an art style that had appeared from the earliest times as child art, or primitive, geometric or Archaic art. Little children use it spontaneously; it is not taught. Does this art style come because we could not learn to draw with representational skill? Why could we not? Is there an immaturity, a physical failure in coordination, as when my left hand cannot cut with right-hand scissors? Or is it a failure to learn a common view, that can be seen when we look at things through another's eyes? A little boy of three years carefully drew himself a picture and then brought it for me to tell him what he had drawn. Yet some young children can draw representationally, can copy the outlines of an object or a drawing.

I could see that the little group who came to my studio to paint or play with clay did not suffer the pain I suffered in trying to get my original work accepted by a publisher or gallery owner: the patients used lines and shapes, colours and forms for themselves alone. They did not suffer for their creativity, in fact they were often happier when they left than when they came, as if relieved of some torment. The torment might well be back again the following week, but for the time spent in creative work they were in a different mood, had seen something new, had made something of their own. Their regular attendance told me that it was important for them to create art.

My pain was caused when my inner, indescribable conviction about the shapes and colours, size and placement of the things I painted came into conflict with my need to reconcile the results of this creative vision with an uncreative and unoriginal market. I wondered if, perhaps, mental patients saw their lives as always in torment of finding life, like my professional life a ceaseless struggle to sustain the certainty of inner vision in an uncomprehending world. Seen in this way, their oddities, their alien moods and madness were their creations, even less acceptable than my pictures and ceramic work. Perhaps paper and pencil, chalk and clay gave them the freedom that their symptoms could not.

In time I came to understand that naturalistic or conventional art was made by those who needed to find a congenial image of external reality. People who become physically ill or disabled need to establish a new place for themselves in the external world, even though, like Peter (Chapter 4), they might not be able to live a physically normal life. When this need was frustrated, it seemed that they, like Joyce (Chapter 7), were measuring their idea against some ideal yardstick that did not allow for their inner vision – the original and inviolable Self that is mirrored in Archaic art.

It seemed that Archaic artists were those who claimed their inner world of sensuous and emotional reality: they made it visible in images that are seen with the inner eye and felt to be more real than the familiar look of perceived reality.

The division into two sorts of art and their relation to two sorts of reality is, of course, a drastic simplification. Many, if not most of patients' works of art presented one style as dominant yet contained elements of others. When these secondary styles were studied it was clear that they formed a continuous circle of styles, as shown in the frontispiece.

When a patient's style changed over a period of time I saw that this reflected a change of attitude towards inner and outer psychic needs; when Peter, for instance, needed to express his inner feelings his style regressed to the Archaic; perhaps a year passed before he began to look for smaller painting panels and, little by little, reduced the scale of his art. Had his choice been limited to the smaller size of his painting area I would have concluded that he found a smaller picture easier to paint but, in fact, they were not so easy, for his control of small movements was very erratic; it was not for reasons of ease or comfort that his paintings changed style, but due to his imaginative vision of space and distance that allowed him to see a panorama, rather than the close view of the Archaic scale.

Mr Pauli (Chapter 2) taught me how little might be needed to provide an adequate area of privacy where creative art could develop; over the year that he drew his faces the change in his style followed the same course as Peter's, from the inner world of Archaic art to the outer reality of a cultural tradition.

A patient's art may move in the opposite, anti-clockwise direction; Sally's art (Chapter 8, circle of styles) did this, for she needed to escape for a while from her sympathetic identification with her mother, expressed in her Traditional Massive art, in order to meet and express the rage and grief of her primary bereavement. I described in my previous book a similar therapeutic regression that occurred briefly during a crisis intervention.

My work with children under the age of six showed me that Archaic art begins with abstract shapes as soon as a child sees his gestures recorded. It seemed strange to think of a two- or three-year-old making abstract symbols (perhaps with saliva, shit or pudding), since we think of this as being a sophisticated form of adult art. It was less surprising when I realized that adults can move round the circle of styles in his or her developing view of life, to return to the Archaic by way of Traditional Linear images translated as calligraphic shapes and reduced finally to the basic form of Circle in Square. The little child had stayed with his sensuous pleasure in shapes and colours.

The inner world would be visualized at first very simply, as an abstract Circle in the centre of a Square symbolizing outer life, but as the child grows and becomes more aware of his needs, the symbolic image is elaborated with identifying attributes. Eventually, the boundary of the Circle becomes faint when inner and outer life blend; the Circle becomes the underlying composition that contains various images shaped by ideas, or space and light.

Once again I asked myself: 'What is going on in us that says to the child "I want to draw", that says to me "You are an artist and you know what art is by doing it"?' How do I recognize art that may be so old that I would find the artist's appearance and speech altogether strange? Is it possible that, from the beginning of life to its end we have a need to find or create images that balance the claims of dual reality and find a place for the Self we experience as inside confirmed in the outer world?

I started to work as a therapist in ignorance of therapy although, by practising as an artist I now see that I was also using it to find myself in my outer world. This brings me finally to the conclusion that creative art is a means of therapy in times when the patient is caught in a conflict between inner and outer life. I see the creative drive as innate, an instinctive means of self-preservation, confirming our individuality and yet stimulating new and further use of the circumstances that life thrusts on us. Those who are well can enjoy the work of other artists and appreciate their visions of integrated life. But those who have become ill and overwhelmed and those who are frightened and angry need a place and time where they can discover the integrating image within themselves.

Glossary of terms

CATEGORIES

Gesture	Use of the body during painting, etc.
Scale	Proportion of detail to area of work, i.e., large scale with few details; small scale with many details
Colour	General effect, e.g., warm, cold, soft, brilliant, etc.
Dimension	Illusion of space or flatness
Design	Organization of the pictorial elements
Orientation	Artist's attitude to the subject and cultural context
Typical subject	Refers to sequences of paintings, etc.
Medium	Oil, gouache, pastel, charcoal, etc.

ART STYLES

Style 1 The Archaic Linear style
Posture and gestures free, arm and wrist.
Large scale, heraldic colour, 2-dimensional, symmetrical design, abstract metaphysical subjects.

Style 2 The Archaic Massive style
Posture/gestures rapid, vivacious arm and wrist movements, brilliant, hot colours, convex effect, voluminous, swirling, emotional appearance.

Style 3 The Traditional Massive style
Tentative gestures, small movements, cool colours, small scale, 3-dimensional illusion of recession, naturalistic, chiaroscopic, spatial relation, detached.

Style 4 The Traditional Linear style
Tense posture, wrist and finger 'writing' movements, local colour, i.e. green for grass, small scale, perspective without spatial illusion, factual, literal, caricatured, fragmented, multiple focal points, literal.

Subject index

Name index